# Meet Me On The Mountain

### Rev Kathryn L Smith

PUBLISHED by
PARABLES
*Earthly Stories with a Heavenly Meaning*

Meet Me On The Mountain
Rev. Kathryn L. Smith
Author of There Is Fire In The Blood

Copyright © Kathryn L. Smith
December, 2016

*Published By Parables*
December, 2016

All Rights Reserved. No part of this book may be reproduced or utilized in any form or by any means, electronic or mechanical, including photocopying, recording, or by any information storage and retrieval system, without permission in writing from the author.

Unless otherwise specified Scripture quotations are taken from the authorized version of the King James Bible.

> ISBN 978-1-945698-49-1
> Printed in the United States of America

Readers should be aware that Internet Web sites offered as citations and/or sources for further information may have been changed or disappeared between the time this was written and when it is read.

# Meet Me On The Mountain

### Rev Kathryn L. Smith

## Table of Contents

10  Meet Me on the Mountain
15  Adam's Loss—Enoch's Gain
21  God in Pursuit of Man
33  Redeemed on Calvary
45  Jesus went to the Mountain—Prayer
57  The Lord is my Portion
63  Ascending Praise and Worship
71  From Mt. Carmel to Mt. Horeb
79  Mt. Sinai
87  Presence Demands Obedience
99  Give Me that Mountain
111  Faith that Works
121  Climbing is Hard
129  Mt. of Transfiguration A Glimpse of the Glory
133  Sitting down on the Path
141  It is Worth the Climb
149  Works Cited

## Acknowledgements

I feel a very deep gratitude to my wonderful husband, William R. Smith II, [Buzz] who loved me all these years and allowed me to follow God's call, even when it meant I was gone preaching or consumed with writing.

I deeply appreciate all those who made me the woman of faith, the minister and the author that I am. I want to especially thank my Pastor Timothy A. Naylor, and those previous Pastors who have shaped and instructed me over the years. I want to honor Pastor Rick Naylor, Pastor Mark Maynard, and Pastor Sherman J. Smith III; these men of faith invested in my spiritual growth and served as shepherds to my soul. I also want to express my gratitude to the men and women whose ministries and books have shaped my faith; some of those names have faded over time, but their truths have become ingrained within my spirit; to all those who taught me and nurtured me, but were not specifically cited in this book—thank you.

Mostly, I want to thank the Lord Jesus Christ who loved me when I was lost, called me when I was nothing and anointed me to do His work. I pray that He will be glorified and lifted high in all I have attempted for Him.

## Meet Me on the Mountain

When I think about mountains, I remember the huge peaks that loomed on the horizon as our family drove toward California. I remember driving for hours with them growing higher and more ominous as we approached them. I also think about them as obstacles, or challenges, or even goals. I think of the massive God who created them like a child playing in the sand. That same God who created us still calls to us, "Come meet me on the Mountain."

It is not the mountain we seek, but something greater in the experience. That place, where obedience and faith come into intimacy with God is the mountain of the Lord. We want to meet Him on that mountain because it is there we see Him, there we commune with Him. It is there we find more of Him. The drive to climb is not just man striving for God; it is an answer to the call. "Meet me on the mountain." God calls out to the heart of man come, draw near to me. **Jeremiah 29:11-13 (KJV)** *11 For I know the thoughts that I think toward you, saith the LORD, thoughts of peace, and not of evil, to give you an expected end. 12 Then shall ye call upon me, and ye shall go and pray unto me, and I will* *hearken unto you. 13 And ye shall seek me, and find me, when ye shall search for me with all your heart.* God has a good plan for us and if we seek Him we will find Him and it.

There is a drive for something within men, to seek out and to conquer. The reason we climb the natural mountain is that it is there waiting, beckoning to man to come and challenge it. The reason we climb the mountain of the Lord is to find Him. We just want the One who made the mountain and who has manifested His presence there. We seek out that high experience with God. We want the experience of men like Moses who had already been in the glory of His presence but was asking for more of God. The Lord is calling us to meet Him on the mountains of faith like Caleb, and Elijah. He is calling us to just come away with Him and hear His voice. He will meet us on the mountain if we will make time to seek Him; God wants His children near.

The Lord spoke to me concerning our time in His presence and He said, "Just stay in my presence a little longer and stay in my favor and grace, stay within my spirit and receive of me. Stay and I will fill you up and make you whole. Stay and I will satisfy that longing in your soul. Come to me and stay here long enough to let my spirit flood your very being and you will finally be free. What you really need is my love and my presence and you can have it if you will just come to me." You will never find all you are looking for in the church service or a prayer meeting or any other gathering of the saints. Yes, He will visit with you there, but what you really need is intimacy and that comes only when you seek Him on your own.

When Elijah was running from Ahab and Jezebel, he was discouraged and frustrated and an angel fed him and then he was urged to meet God on the mountain. **1 Kings 19:11-19 (KJV)** *11 And he said, <u>Go forth, and stand upon the mount before the LORD</u>. And, behold, the LORD passed by, and a great and strong wind rent the mountains, and brake in pieces the rocks before the LORD; but the LORD was not in the wind: and after the wind an earthquake; but the LORD was not in the earthquake: 12 And after the earthquake a fire; but the LORD was not in the fire: and after the fire <u>a still small voice.</u> 13 And it was so, when Elijah heard it, that he wrapped His face in His mantle, and went out, and stood in the entering in of the cave.* That voice was just a whisper in the spirit. God does not always come in a spectacular way. He is looking for those who will come away with Him and stand on the mount to hear His voice and obey it.

Never seek the spectacular when what you really want is the One who gave you supernatural life. No single manifestation will satisfy the heart of man. We need the presence of God. No miracle or event is worth what even a moment in His presence is to our hearts. Kenneth Copeland made this phrase his motto, "One word from God can change you forever." He was right. Jesus redeemed you from sin for the purpose of fellowship. Communion with God is priceless.

We only want Him; we want that place of harmony and intimacy that comes from being where He is. God promised Israel to go with them through the desert until they reached the Promised Land. He held out hope to them and a land of milk and honey in which to live. It was God's presence that was their real treasure. As His covenant partners, they were walking in the shadow of God day in and day out. They were not facing their enemies alone. It was God's presence that they were called to. He wanted them to be near Him, but they did not see that it was God Himself that they sought out. A deep personal relationship with the Lord was offered to them. That covenant relationship was more valuable than the land. He has told us this world is not our home but we can stand in faith that we too have a calling to inherit more than just heaven. The Lord is our portion, our inheritance.

You can have the life you always wanted in the spirit, but it will not come casually or accidentally. You will have to seek God. You will do some climbing, pursuing Him and desiring Him. It takes time alone with Him. God wants a people who will pursue Him with passion. God wants more than a revival, more than great worship, or new buildings. He will give us that, but what we really need is His presence. If we will position ourselves to hear from the Lord, we will. If we will quiet our minds, our spirits will grow sensitive to Him. **Deuteronomy 4:29 (KJV)** *29 But if from thence thou shalt seek the LORD thy God, thou shalt find Him, if thou seek Him with all thy heart and with all thy soul.*

## Adam's Loss ~ Enoch's Gain

When the Creator of the earth chose to include a race of beings greater than animals, it must have been because He wanted more than animals could give Him. God created man with the capacity and the desire to communicate and to fellowship. Man was created with a hunger to walk in unity with the One who made him. God, not man, was the author of that loving relationship.

**Genesis 1:26-27 (KJV)** *26 And God said, Let us make man in our image, after our likeness: and let them have dominion over the fish of the sea, and over the fowl of the air, and over the cattle, and over all the earth, and over every creeping thing that creepeth upon the earth. 27 So God created man in his own image, in the image of God created he him; male and female created he them.*

**Genesis 2: 7 (KJV)** *7 And the LORD God formed man of the dust of the ground, and breathed into his nostrils the breath of life; and man became a living soul.* God molded him; He placed His hands all over the external shell of man. Then God took life from within Him, and breathed it into

Adam. The man had an essence of God inside him, he became a living spirit. He was, like his Creator, an eternal spirit, with a soul that could freely think and speak. Man was always intended to be God's reflection on the earth. It was that sameness that opened a door of fellowship. God desired and initiated relationship with His creation. It has always been in the heart of God to fellowship freely with mankind. For a while that is exactly what happened. Day by day, man walked with the Lord. They spoke with one another sharing whatever was in their hearts.

We know that Adam and Eve lived for an extended period of time in perfect communion with their Creator. He gave them all they needed, and fellowshipped with them daily. They had dominion over the whole of creation. God gave them total provision in a perfect world, and only one restriction. **Genesis 2:16-17 (KJV)** *16 And the LORD God commanded the man, saying, Of every tree of the garden thou mayest freely eat: 17 But of the tree of the knowledge of good and evil, thou shalt not eat of it: for in the day that thou eatest thereof thou shalt surely die.* There were two trees in the midst of the Garden. There was the one forbidden, but there was also that tree of life. [Genesis 3:22] I believe it is the same "Tree of Life" mentioned in Rev. 2:7, and Rev. 22:2 and Rev. 22:14. If Adam had chosen that tree prior to the forbidden tree, he could have lived forever in a state of unity with God.

There came a day when they chose their own way, and partook of the forbidden tree, ending their perfect harmony with God. "To rebel in an act of disobedience that declared independence from Him was to disconnect with the source of life and plunge into death." (Smith p.27) They had not broken some manmade law or an arbitrary rule of conduct, they had refused God as Lord, and they had turned away from union with Him. Every man from that time forward would long for the kind of unity they lost. God did not want man to live forever in his fallen state, so Adam was driven from the paradise he had known. That separation was devastating.

"Historic Jewish writings tell of the depression Adam suffered after being driven from the garden. The weight of it was almost unbearable." (Bevere, p.11) For generations, no one really walked with God. Then came Enoch, the great, great, great, great, grandson of Adam, and he wanted what Adam lost. Adam was 687 years old when Enoch who was then 65, began walking with God. Surely, Adam had shared with Enoch. He would have mentioned the times of refreshing that came from his walks with the Lord. He must have told Enoch what it was like to know God and fellowship with Him—to inquire of Him and find an answer to every question. They had named the animals and stars together. God had given Adam a wife, created from his own body. Adam had been offered the comfort of her love and companionship. Adam had shared sunrise and sunset with God and it was a paradise there in the Garden when they were in perfect unity. There was still a passion within Adam and all of mankind to have that relationship with God. If there were hundreds of years of fellowship before the fall, there were many memories to draw upon.

All Adam shared inspired a hunger in Enoch who then purposed to walk with that One who created everything on earth. **Genesis 5:23-24 (KJV)** *23 And all the days of Enoch were three hundred sixty and five years: 24 And Enoch walked with God: and he was not; for God took him.* When we determine to seek God, something changes in our spirits. Enoch made a quality decision to know God. The heart of Enoch was so tender toward God that He responded. I imagine their fellowship, growing over the years. No one after Adam had ever communed like Enoch with God. According to the Scriptures, Enoch walked with God for 300 years. Three hundred years full of fellowship was only a beginning when placed in perspective with eternity. It may have been as long as Adam and Eve held to God, we have no way of knowing. It was a unique relationship. He must have experienced numerous precious moments with God. For the first 243 of those years, Adam was still alive. I wonder if he shared his encounters with the elderly Adam. Enoch, who learned to love God by listening to Adam, may have come home to inspire Adam afresh.

**Hebrews 11:5-6 (KJV)** *5 By faith Enoch was translated that he should not see death; and was not found, because God had translated him: for before his translation he had this testimony, that he pleased God. 6 But without faith it is impossible to please him: for he that cometh to God must believe that he is, and that he is a rewarder of them that diligently seek him.* If we look at those two Scriptures together, the text infers that Enoch diligently sought for the presence of God, and found Him. They were close to one another. Their relationship grew deeper day by day until they could no longer be separated. In my mind Enoch's walk was close enough to God that one day God just said, "Come home with me." There have only been two men who never tasted of death, one was Enoch and the other was Elijah. Both had a reputation of walking in deep union with God. It is beyond our understanding for an Old Testament, unsaved man to reach the status that Enoch found. According to John Bevere "His walk with God produced a powerful and effective ministry, but it was his burning desire to know God intimately that pleased the Lord. He had touched the longing in God's heart, an intimate relationship with Him, the way He longs for us." (Bevere, p. 13) God is still looking for men and women who will diligently, passionately seek Him. He wants us to walk in absolute unity with the whole of the Trinity.

Adam had lost so much—all men shared his loss; they were disconnected until the time of Christ. If Enoch could find that place of fellowship with God, surely we can find it, now that Jesus has made a way. "We were created to dwell with Him in reality, not theory alone. Until we experience the fullness of this we should never be satisfied." (Bevere, p. 50) God's deep desire to fellowship with us and our hunger for that lost presence, were both meant to draw us back to what Adam lost, and what Enoch found.

**Psalm 27:8 (KJV)** *8 When thou saidst, Seek ye my face; my heart said unto thee, Thy face, LORD, will I seek.* "God is seeking those who will hear His call to a life of Worship." (Bevere, p. 119) God calls to His beloved, "Come away with me—meet me on the mountain," and hopefully we respond by taking intentional steps to walk closer day by day.

1 John 4: 10 (KJV) *10 Herein is love, not that we loved God, but that he loved us,*

1 John 4:19 *19 We love him, because he first loved us.*

## God in Pursuit of Man

God saw something of such value in mankind that He made a way for us. To understand any part of our own climb, we have to start with relationship and we must be aware that God loved us first. Mankind was a mess. Men sinned continually and even the best of men failed God, but for some reason God still wanted fellowship and communion with mankind. God was willing to go to extreme measures to have real fellowship with us. There was a longing in heaven for man and a longing in man for God. The sin gulf was so wide that only divinity could bridge it. So Jesus left heaven and entered into our world in order to bring us closer to Him. He willingly became an offering for sinful man.

**1 John 4:19 (KJV)** *19 We love Him, because he first loved us.* There was nothing in mankind that should have been worth redeeming with the richest treasure of heaven. Jesus saw something in us that He was willing to die for. That is more than we could have hoped and definitely more than we deserved. When man was unlovely, God saw us with the eyes of love. My granddaughter taught me about seeing through love when she was just a little girl.

Mackenzie had a doll named Micah. Micah had soft rubber arms and legs and a cloth body. She was stuffed with rags and that is appropriate because she looked ragged. She was permanently stained and always looked dirty. I used every cleaning product on the market, bleach, Ajax, window cleaner, antibacterial bathroom cleaner, hydrogen peroxide and even steel wool, nothing could get her presentable. Once her leg got ripped off and Mackenzie was inconsolable, so I had to do surgery. Micah lost her cuteness and her original clothes long ago. We dressed her in newborn diapers and baby clothes from yard sales. I would put her in long sleeves and pants if it was my choice because it would cover the places where her cloth body joined her rubber arms and some of her other imperfections. Mackenzie found cute summer dresses and let all of her flaws show. She was never ashamed of Micah. We tried buying a substitute that looked exactly like the original doll but Mackenzie would have nothing to do with it. I am now the proud owner of that substitute. Mackenzie took Micah to school and church and shopping and outside to play and she always slept with her. Micah meant so much to Mackenzie that I pushed her in shopping carts and strollers, and she used a car seat. To Kenzie she was perfect, wonderful and beautiful. To be honest, Kenzie is 20 and we still know exactly where Micah is.

I once read about another little girl like Mackenzie whose doll was old and damaged, but dearly loved. When that girl was grown, no one had the heart to throw her doll out. The doll was no longer beautiful but the love connection was strong. So, the girl's mother put the doll away in the attic. When her daughter was married with a little girl of her own on the way, the mother remembered the cherished doll. One day she and her daughter decided to try to restore her old tattered doll. They failed to make any real progress on their own. Later they sent the doll to a "doll hospital" where it received new clothes and new hair and some reconstructive surgery. When the doll came back they unpacked it together and her mother said, "I forgot she ever looked like that." Her daughter said, "I never saw her any other way." She looked at her doll through loving eyes.

All of us are just a little ragged and broken too. We are stained and tattered and you would think no one would love us, but you would be wrong. The whole time we were stained by sin and dirtied by the world, God saw us for the beautiful person we were created to be. When we were unlovely we were never unloved. When we looked like lost causes, God still saw us made in His image. He saw all the potential in us, and His love gave us value.

**Romans 5:6-8 (KJV)** *6 For when we were yet without strength, in due time Christ died for the ungodly. 7 For scarcely for a righteous man will one die: yet peradventure for a good man some would even dare to die. 8 But God commendeth His love toward us, in that, while we were yet sinners, Christ died for us.* "We have done nothing to merit His love and pursuit. For when we were still decrepit, lost sinners—enemies—He sought us out. He saw in us what only His love could see. He saw treasures in the midst of corruption, sin and depravity. He purchased as precious what many considered worth little or even worthless. He saw beyond our state and saw what only His grace could produce." (Bevere, p. 22) That is amazing love.

**James 4:8 (KJV)** *8 Draw nigh to God, and he will draw nigh to you.* How good it is to know we are welcome in the presence of the Almighty. "Stop for a moment and ponder this: the Creator of the universe, the earth and all of its inhabitants, requests your presence. Not only your presence, but He desires to be intimately close, for we are told He is a God who is passionate about His relationship with you." (Bevere, p.2) God longs for fellowship with you.

When Jesus walked this earth, those who were most aware of their failure and ragged edges, were also some of those most open to His love. Among them was the woman caught in adultery and thrown at His feet. To whom He showed great mercy and said, *"Neither do I condemn you, go and sin no more."* (John 8:11) Another of those broken women was the Samaritan woman at the well. (John 4:4-26) My favorite one was the woman who poured out her heart to Him in a display of worship that still inspires passion. That was the woman with the alabaster box. Each of these three came to the place where the depth of her sin was exposed and she was standing in the presence of a holy Jesus. He had the opportunity to reject and condemn her or set her free. Just like them, I was caught in sin, guilty, with no case to plead when He forgave me. He who was so holy saw something of worth in what the world called worthless.

**Luke 7:36-39 (KJV)** *36 And one of the Pharisees desired him that he would eat with him. And he went into the Pharisee's house, and sat down to meat.* By all accounts Simon was probably a decent man. He was a Pharisee so he knew the law and probably kept it. He was better prepared to stand before God than most of the men in town. He was somewhat wealthy and though he did not honor Jesus as the Christ, he was at least curious about this teacher. *37 And, behold, a woman in the city, which was a sinner, when she knew that Jesus sat at meat in the Pharisee's house, brought an alabaster box of ointment, 38 And stood at his feet.* She was most likely a prostitute. The name they called her was much stronger than I would be comfortable saying. It carried with it shame and humiliation that we cannot comprehend. Here she is in the very presence of the Son of God. The contrast was lost on no one. It was scandalous to everyone in the room that she would come in there uninvited, unwelcome, and of shameful reputation. She just walked up to Jesus and touched Him. He never withdrew from her touch. The only one who had a right to judge her was the Lord. He was also the only one who was not offended. She had not always been dirty and vile; there was a time she was someone's little girl. She had long since lost her reputation and her virtue. She is no longer the one that people hold out hope for or dreams and plans for a future or a family. It had been a long time since she was welcome in polite society. The whole room was full of men who despised her and she probably hated herself. The Scripture says she just barged in but she also brought an alabaster box of ointment. That box and the perfume inside would cost about a year's wages. It was not a small offering. It is likely that she had used tiny amounts of this or a similar perfume in her profession. Women of disrepute often used rich perfumes and oils and here she is pouring out her shameful past in an act of worship that only a truly repentant heart can offer. She cried the whole time she ministered to the Lord. *38 And stood at His feet behind Him weeping, and began to wash His feet with tears, and did wipe them with the hairs of her head, and kissed His feet, and anointed them with the ointment.* Maybe she was thinking of how she had earned the money that bought that perfume, or maybe she remembered the cherished little girl she used to be and thought about how disgusting her life had become. She was probably pretty but men only looked at her with lust. No one looked at her heart and loved her for who she was inside. She was just a convenience for men who wanted her body for a few hours. Maybe she was thinking of how ugly her sin was and how much she wanted to be clean and beautiful again. As she wept she did something unorthodox, she took down her hair. It was a violation of social custom for respectable women to do that, but she was not respectable. She had let down her hair many times as a prostitute, and each time it was another wound to her own heart and another scar and stain on her own soul. This time it was an act of homage, to dry the feet her tears had bathed. She let down her hair this one last time out of love and respect for the one man worthy of her love and admiration.

She wept and bathed His feet in her remorse. Her deep sorrow and shame overcame her. *38 And stood at his feet behind him weeping, and began to wash his feet with tears, and did wipe them with the hairs of her head, and kissed his feet, and anointed them with the ointment.* I can almost hear her heart cry out, when her tears hit His dirty feet. She was not only wiping away the dust from the road, but maybe she thought her tears were too vile to touch Him. *39 Now when the Pharisee which had bidden him saw it, he spake within himself, saying, This man, if he were a prophet, would have known who and what manner of woman this is that toucheth him: for she is a sinner.* It had to take all her courage to walk in there knowing the whispers and stares she would encounter. She knew she was unwelcome, but she had to do what she came for. I am sure she stood behind the Lord because she feared to face this holy man. When she finally did look Jesus in the eyes, she saw love and compassion. Simon had none of that for her. His lack of spiritual vision meant he did not see the woman or Jesus as he should. He was waiting for Jesus to denounce and rebuke her but instead Jesus forgave her. He forgave us too.

**Luke 7:40-50 (KJV)** *40 And Jesus answering said unto him, Simon, I have somewhat to say unto thee. And he saith, Master, say on. 41 There was a certain creditor which had two debtors: the one owed five hundred pence, and the other fifty. 42 And when they had nothing to pay, he frankly* *forgave them both. Tell me therefore, which of them will love him most? 43 Simon answered and said, I suppose that he, to whom he forgave most. And he said unto him, Thou hast rightly judged. 44 And he turned to the woman, and said unto Simon, Seest thou this woman?* Of course Simon could see her, but he did not look at her as Jesus did. He never saw the treasure within her. He quickly judged and dismissed her. Simon did not see Jesus either, not as she did. *I entered into thine house, thou gavest me no water for my feet: but she hath washed my feet with tears, and wiped them with the hairs of her head. 45 Thou gavest me no kiss: but this woman since the time I came in hath not ceased to kiss my feet. 46 My head with oil thou didst not anoint: but this woman hath anointed my feet with ointment.* In every household someone was designated to wash the feet of guests, usually the lowest servant. It was always customary to greet a friend or an honored guest with a kiss on both cheeks and to anoint them with inexpensive olive oil. It was common courtesy, but none of it was extended to the Lord in this house. They knelt down at the table with none of the customary washings or greetings. Simon had disrespected the Lord. *47 Wherefore I say unto thee, Her sins, which are many, are forgiven; for she loved much: but to whom little is forgiven, the same loveth little. 48 And he said unto her, Thy sins are forgiven. 49 And they that sat at meat with Him began to say within themselves, Who is this that forgiveth sins also? 50 And he said to the woman, Thy faith hath saved thee; go in peace.* For some reason Simon had invited Jesus come, but he did not honor Him as a prophet or even a teacher. In his pride, Simon thought he was better than any common sinner. Simon did not realize that he was as damaged as that disgraceful woman and he too needed forgiveness. I am sure he was outraged to think Jesus would honor a prostitute over him. That woman came in an attitude of true repentance and sorrow for her sin. She had determined to worship Jesus.

She had come with a heart of unlimited devotion, and humble adoration. She had closed the door on her past, and opened herself up to public outrage and social disgrace in order to minister to Jesus. She had placed herself at His feet and she was rewarded for her love.

Jesus saw that sad broken woman differently from those who looked in the natural. He saw her as beloved by the Father, damaged beyond recognition by the world, but still valuable and beautiful to God. He saw her with the eyes of love. **1 John 4:8-10 (KJV)** *8 He that loveth not knoweth not God; for God is love. 9 In this was manifested the love of God toward us, because that God sent his only begotten Son into the world, that we might live through him. 10 Herein is love, not that we loved God, but that he loved us, and sent his Son to be the propitiation for our sins.* God loved us first and that motivated Him to save us.

Jesus never said that her sin did not matter, what He did say was that it was not going to stop His love. He became sin so that it could no longer hold us prisoner. **Song of Songs 8:6 (KJV)** *...for love is strong as death;* In fact love for mankind was so strong that it walked through the earth in the form of a man and overcame death. God's love is limitless. Even though man is dirty and worn and broken God still loves us. God is not against us, in fact, He is for us. **Romans 8:31-33 (KJV)** *31 What shall we then say to these things? If God be for us, who can be against us? 32 He that spared not His own Son, but delivered Him up for us all, how shall he not with Him also freely give us all things? 33 Who shall lay any thing to the charge of God's elect? It is God that justifieth.*

Have you ever had a child hold out both arms as far as they would stretch and say, "I love you this much?" I heard a story about that once. The mother and her son would say that all the time. One day they were washing the car and that little boy opened the trunk and proceeded to hose down everything inside. The carpet was wet, but worse than that so were her expensive college textbooks. Her twenty page research paper and everything else in her backpack were ruined. The cake and a beautifully wrapped birthday present for her best friend lay in a puddle. Maps and a photo album and mom's favorite coat were all in that trunk and now lay soaked. When the little boy saw his mother's face, I am sure he had instant understanding that the wages of this particular sin warranted death. He held out his arms trembling, "I love you this much." Some of those things would dry over time and some were destroyed. If she took all the money from his piggy bank it would never be enough for the books or the gift that was lost. She did what mothers have done for years. She held out her arms and said it back. "I love you this much." That mother acted out of compassion; she took him into her arms, forgave him, and assumed his debt.

That is what Jesus did. He stretched out His arms and let men nail them to the cross. That was God saying I love you this much, no more sin, no judgment, no guilt or regrets. Every demand of justice was paid and you are free to love Him who loved you first. The cross openly shows how much God hated sin, but also how very much He loved mankind.

**Psalm 103:8-13 (KJV)** *8 The LORD is merciful and gracious, slow to anger, and plenteous in mercy. 9 He will not always chide: neither will he keep his anger forever. 10 He hath not dealt with us after our sins; nor rewarded us according to our iniquities. 11 For as the heaven is high above the earth, so great is his mercy toward them that fear* *him. 12 As far as the east is from the west, so far hath he removed our transgressions from us. 13 Like as a father pitieth his children, so the LORD pitieth them that fear him.*

God did not wait for man to seek Him. Instead God made a way and actively pursued us that we might be free and able to receive His love. He has called us to Himself, purchased us for Himself. He became flesh like we are flesh because He wanted more than anything to have us in perfect union with the whole of the Trinity. Jesus came here knowing He would be rejected and abused and He willingly poured out His own lifeblood to purchase our souls. Such passion on His part should inspire us to love Him.

**Psalm 84:1-2 (KJV)** *1 How amiable are thy tabernacles, O LORD of hosts! 2 My soul longeth, yea, even fainteth for the courts of the LORD: my heart and my flesh crieth out for the living God.* The heart of man and the heart of God both want intimacy. God is looking for hungry souls who will seek Him until they find Him. It is His will that we press into His presence and live our whole life there. Each time we meet with God, we are changed by the encounter. The presence of the Lord always produces greater revelation of His nature and character. We know Him by climbing until we are standing face to face with Him.

Deeply imbedded in salvation is the idea that we not only have eternity with the Lord someday in heaven, but that we are carriers of eternity here and now. He is a living God who wants us to know Him while we are living in the earth. He intends for us to have an abiding communion with Him. He chose us as His own children. What kind of a father would leave us abandoned after adopting us? Our heavenly Father is eager to talk with us, and share in every aspect of our lives. He is calling us to come, calling us to meet with Him. He wants us to really know Him and experience His love. **Romans 5:6-11 (KJV)** *6 For when we were yet without strength, in due time Christ died for the ungodly. 7 For scarcely for a righteous man will one die: yet peradventure for a good man some would even dare to die. 8 But God commendeth His love toward us, in that, while we were yet sinners, Christ died for us. 9 Much more then, being now justified by His blood, we shall be saved from wrath through Him. 10 For if, when we were enemies, we were reconciled to God by the death of His Son, much more, being reconciled, we shall be saved by His life. 11 And not only so, but we also joy in God through our Lord Jesus Christ, by whom we have now received the atonement.* Look at just that last verse in the New Living Testament. **Romans 5:11 (NLT)** *11 So now we can rejoice in our wonderful new relationship with God because our Lord Jesus Christ has made us friends of God.* He sought us out, died so we would never face the penalty of death and made us His own. He calls us the friends of God, and then calls upon us to come and fellowship with Him.

John 3:16 *16 For God so loved the world, that he gave his only begotten Son, that whosoever believeth in him should not perish, but have everlasting life.*

## Redeemed on Calvary

Jesus came in order to free a fallen race; the world was full of lost people. His intent was to climb a hill called Calvary for the very purpose of offering His own blood upon the cross. It was a hill we could not climb. His life was the only acceptable offering for sin. Sin must be judged and death must be defeated. Either the whole of mankind was destroyed or God Himself would lay down a life that would redeem all of man. There was no other way for mankind to be made right with God the Father.

"There can be no fellowship of the type that the Father craves unless man is utterly free from sin consciousness and free from the fear of Satan's domain." (Kenyon, p. 81) That means we have to know we are saved from our old sin nature and welcome in the presence of God. **John 3:16-17 (KJV)** *16 For God so loved the world, that he gave his only begotten Son, that whosoever believeth in him should not perish, but have everlasting life. 17 For God sent not his Son into the world to condemn the world; but that the world through him might be saved.*

The reason God redeemed mankind is that God's love was stronger than man's rebellion. His love moved Him to act by sending His Son to buy us out of bondage with a sacrificial offering of His own blood. Once forgiven, man was ready to join God's family. **Job 33:26 (KJV)** *26 He shall pray unto God, and he will be favourable unto him: and he shall see his face with joy: for he will render unto man his righteousness.* Jesus became sin so we would be made the righteousness of God in Christ. God made us righteous so we could come back to Him.

He cleansed us by virtue of the sacrifice He planned from the foundation of the earth. **Hebrews 2:14-17 (KJV)** *14 Forasmuch then as the children are partakers of flesh and blood, he also himself likewise took part of the same; that through death he might destroy him that had the power of death, that is, the devil; 15 And deliver them who through fear of death were all their lifetime subject to bondage. 16 For verily he took not on him the nature of angels; but he took on him the seed of Abraham. 17 Wherefore in all things it behoved him to be made like unto his brethren, that he might be a merciful and faithful high priest in things pertaining to God, to make reconciliation for the sins of the people.* Jesus did not come as a conquering king. He did not even come as an adult. He made Himself vulnerable; He came as an infant. He was fully dependent upon the damaged human race. He faced all that we face growing up. He saw poverty and need and sorrow just like we do. He walked upon this earth with all of the same feelings and frailties that we have. Jesus knew what it was to be weary and even tempted, but He never succumbed to sin. He understood the whole of what it means to be human in a fallen world. He came to remove the curse that fell upon Adam's entire race.

Jesus, our substitute died that we could live. **Hebrews 9:22 (KJV)** *22 And almost all things are by the law purged with blood; and without shedding of blood is no remission.* We are blood bought, ransomed from sin by the blood offering of the Holy Son of God. "Life itself is spiritual, but it must have a physical carrier, and this carrier is the blood." (Whyte p. 14) If just any human blood of a righteous man would do, Abel would have put an end to sin and the death that came with it. Regular blood, like that in Abel was never sufficient. It could never satisfy the demands of justice. The blood in his veins was tainted, contaminated by sin. Even though he had not personally rebelled against God in the Garden, his father had. The penalty for sin and the corruption that accompanied it was passed down through every child of Adam. Blood is the carrier for human life, but it can also carry spiritual life or death. When Adam sinned, mankind was forever changed; sin was passed on to every generation. **1 Corinthians 15:22 (KJV)** *22 For as in Adam all die, even so in Christ shall all be made alive.* Life and death were in the blood. No man born from Adam's race could possibly be our redeemer. Since Jesus was not conceived by any human father, we know that the blood in Him was uncontaminated by the sin of Adam. The life of God was in the blood of Jesus and once shed it could be transfused into any willing vessel.

When the world judged Jesus worthy of death on the cross, the scene was set for the whole of mankind to die in Him and be redeemed by Him. **Galatians 2:20 (KJV)** *20 I am crucified with Christ: nevertheless I live; yet not I, but Christ liveth in me: and the life which I now live in the flesh I live by the faith of the Son of God, who loved me, and gave Himself for me.* The price was paid, the gift was given. Salvation was available to every man. In Christ, the old man of sin died and gave birth to a new life in the old shell. Man was infused with the righteousness of God. He identified with us and we partook of His death and then eternal life. When Jesus overcame the grave, mankind was resurrected as well.

This is what we know of the external sacrifice on the cross. **John 19:17-18 (KJV)** *And they took Jesus, and led him away. 17 And he bearing His cross went forth into a place called the place of a skull, which is called in the Hebrew Golgotha: 18 Where they crucified him, and two other with him, on either side one, and Jesus in the midst.* He climbed Mount Calvary carrying the weight of our sin and the wood for His execution. Jesus said "I love you this much." He stretched out His arms and they hammered nails into His hands and feet. If He placed all of the weight of His body on His feet, He could relieve His dislocated shoulders and reduce the pain in His hands. He could gasp for a breath and then the torture of His whole weight on those nail pierced feet would be too much. Jesus would drop again, jarring and tearing at His wounds. He hung on the cross for hours, taunted and reviled, struggling for every breath.

**Mark 15:37-39 (KJV)** *37 And Jesus cried with a loud voice, and gave up the ghost. 38 And the veil of the temple was rent in twain from the top to the bottom. 39 And when the centurion, which stood over against him, saw that he so cried out, and gave up the ghost, he said, Truly this man was the Son of God.* The saving blood of God's sacrifice fell from the hands and feet that were pierced for us; the droplets rained down upon the soldiers below. Holy blood gushed from His side. The blood was shed, the price was paid; once and for all justice was satisfied. The redemption of man was complete. Jesus spoke the same words that the High Priest spoke when the last acceptable lamb was brought to be slain in the temple courtyard. "It is finished." He did not whisper it in defeat, but He shouted it in victory over sin.

**John 19:33-34 (KJV)** *33 But when they came to Jesus, and saw that he was dead already, they brake not his legs: 34 But one of the soldiers with a spear pierced his side, and forthwith came there out blood and water he said, Truly this man was the Son of God.*

We also know these facts from the prophet Isaiah. **Isaiah 53:4-12 (KJV)** *4 Surely he hath borne our griefs, and carried our sorrows: yet we did esteem him stricken, smitten of God, and afflicted. 5 But he was wounded for our transgressions, he was bruised for our iniquities: the chastisement of our peace was upon him;* Every intentional rebellion, careless thought, wrong action and all our failure was laid on Him. The death of Christ would bring peace and communion back to humanity. *and with his stripes we are healed. 6 All we like sheep have gone astray; we have turned every one to his own way; and the LORD hath laid on him the iniquity of us all.* The whole of Adam's sin, and yours and mine were embodied by Jesus. He became our substitute sacrifice. *7 He was oppressed, and he was afflicted, yet he opened not his mouth: he is brought as a lamb to the slaughter, and as a sheep before her shearers is dumb, so he openeth not His mouth. 8 He was taken from prison and from judgment: and who shall declare His generation? for he was cut off out of the land of the living: for the transgression of my people was he stricken. 9 And he made His grave with the wicked, and with the rich in his death; because he had done no violence, neither was any deceit in his mouth.* Jesus suffered humiliation, pain and death. He did not deserve to die. He had never sinned. He was guilty of love, nothing more. He was taken to prison, falsely accused and condemned by the

Jewish Sanhedrin and the Roman government. That made Jesus a sacrifice for both Jews and Gentiles. All the sin of mankind was judged. After Jesus died, they placed His body in a borrowed tomb. *10 Yet it pleased the LORD to bruise him; he hath put him to grief: when thou shalt make his soul an offering for sin, he shall see his seed, he shall prolong his days, and the pleasure of the LORD shall prosper in his hand. 11 He shall see of the travail of his soul, and shall be satisfied: by his knowledge shall my righteous servant justify many; for he shall bear their iniquities. 12 Therefore will I divide him a portion with the great, and he shall divide the spoil with the strong; because he hath poured out his soul unto death: and he was numbered with the transgressors; and he bare the sin of many, and made intercession for the transgressors.* There was and is great freedom for mankind because of what Jesus suffered in our stead. That redemption is ours for the asking.

When we choose to be born again, we enter into covenant with God. Each of us stands in faith believing: "All of my sins are forgiven. I have confessed them all. God has forgiven them all. The blood of Jesus Christ cleanses me from all unrighteousness. I am justified—just-as-if-I'd never sinned." (Prince, p. 128) **Hebrews 10:17 (KJV)** *17 And their sins and iniquities will I remember no more.* God has decided not to hold you accountable, your past sins are forgiven and He will not let them affect His relationship toward you. As you trust in what Jesus did for you, you can come boldly to the throne of grace.

We come alone, with nothing to offer as an excuse for our sin. We come with no offering except the one God provided. That blood opens the door into fellowship with God, joining us together in perfect unity. **1 Corinthians 6:17 (KJV)** *17 But he that is joined unto the Lord is one spirit.*

"Jesus is God coming to where we are, joining us in our lost condition without being lost Himself, taking to Himself our death and carrying us out in His resurrection. We now must be united to Him, partake of His life and strength, and be taken into intimate fellowship with Him where He is." (Smith p. 138) The Hope of the World was sent to die for us. There was enough power in the blood of Jesus to wash clean every fallen soul. God willed for all of us to choose to accept His immeasurable gift. **1 Timothy 2:4-6 (KJV)** *4 Who will have all men to be saved, and to come unto the knowledge of the truth. 5 For there is one God, and one mediator between God and men, the man Christ Jesus; 6 Who gave Himself a ransom for all, to be testified in due time.* Jesus is forever the bridge between God and man. Since He was the perfect representative of both the Godhead and humanity, He could reach from the one to the other, with the intent of reuniting them.

Communion with God demands a joining together. All of our fellowship with the Father is based on relationship that is mutually desired and accepted. We want to be with God and He wants to be with us. Love is not just aware, it pays attention. We have seen the stereotype a thousand times. A man and his wife are sitting at the breakfast table. She is talking and he is reading the paper. After a while she says, "You haven't heard a word I said." Of course he says he can repeat every word. The point is not did he hear the words; the point is she wants his attention. God wants your attention too. It is not enough that you can repeat His words; He wants what that wife wants. Stop everything else and look at me. Give me your undivided attention for a little while. God paid dearly to enter into a holy union with us and He wants the intimacy that should accompany that union.

Anytime we sin, we damage or break the union we have formed. That broken fellowship hinders our faith. "There can be no growth in faith, or growth in grace, or growth in knowledge, or growth in joy, with broken fellowship." (Kenyon, p. 88) Sin consciousness keeps us from drawing near to God. The devil would have you to walk around feeling like a failure, but you are the righteousness of God, His own beloved child through Christ Jesus. You have been born again and are free to enter into His presence. Jesus was our atonement. I have heard it preached that He was the way to 'at-one-ment' the making of our soul united with the soul of God in such a way that we become one. When God says He wants us to know Him, He uses Strong's Hebrew word #3045 *yada.* That word means to know intimately, like when Adam knew Eve and brought forth a son. It depicts understanding, unity, experience with and a seeing of one another. The Scriptures tell us we should no longer fear punishment from God, because the Lord provided for our oneness. **Romans 8:1-4 (KJV)** *1 There is therefore now no condemnation to them which are in Christ Jesus, who walk not after the flesh, but after the Spirit. 2 For the law of the Spirit of life in Christ Jesus hath made me free from the law of sin and death. 3 For what the law could not do, in that it was weak through the flesh, God sending His own Son in the likeness of sinful flesh, and for sin, condemned sin in the flesh: 4 That the righteousness of the law might be fulfilled in us, who walk not after the flesh, but after the Spirit.* How freeing it is to lay down the weight of sin and walk with Jesus who loved us so much.

Why do people struggle with their spiritual relationship? What is it that makes prayer and faith so foreign? Part of it is a sense of unworthiness, but mostly it is a lack of confidence in God and what He has spoken. "The Prayer Problem is a problem of Faith; and Faith is a problem of the integrity of the Word, of the ability of God to stand back of His promises or statements of fact in the Word." (Kenyon, p. 104) Everything in us must determine that the Word of God is true and if it is, we have access to it through the Lord Jesus Christ who died to make us eligible for all of its benefits. **2 Corinthians 5:17-21 (KJV)** *17 Therefore if any man be in Christ, he is a new creature: old things are passed away; behold, all things are ecome new. 18 And all things are of God, who hath reconciled us to himself by Jesus Christ, and hath given to us the ministry of reconciliation; 19 To wit, that God was in Christ, reconciling the world unto himself, not imputing their trespasses unto them; and hath committed unto us the word of reconciliation. 20 Now then we are ambassadors for Christ, as though God did beseech you by us: we pray you in Christ's stead, be ye reconciled to God. 21 For he hath made him to be sin for us, who knew no sin; that we might be made the righteousness of God in Him.* We know that our old man is dead and buried. We died on the cross with Jesus. We ravaged the depths of hell and rose victorious with Jesus and now have access into the very presence of God. "Everything that Jesus did is accredited to us. The entire substitutionary work of Christ was for us. He didn't conquer Satan for Himself. He didn't put sin away for Himself. He didn't suffer the judgment that would have fallen upon the sinner for Himself. But He suffered it on our behalf, and we have entered into His victory; it is accredited to us. So Satan now is a defeated enemy...Every demon knows that you, the recreated one, are his master." (Kenyon, p. 106) His death, attributed to us, makes us powerful and confident.

Faith is acting as if the word of God is unquestionably true and the work of Jesus made you righteous and heir to everything spoken in it. "Your fear to act upon the Word is unbelief gaining the ascendency." (Kenyon, p. 117) You demand that fear bow its knee to the blood of Jesus, and His holy Word. You recognize your sonship and relationship. You determine to live according to the truth of the Bible. You live through the conferred righteousness that came from Jesus, not your own sense of earned righteousness. You base your confidence in who He is and all He did. **2 Corinthians 10:5 (KJV)** *5 Casting down imaginations, and every high thing that exalteth itself against the knowledge of God, and bringing into captivity every thought to the obedience of Christ;* As a believer, you deal with the flesh and give place to God above all else. **Romans 6:6-14 (KJV)** *6 Knowing this, that our old man is crucified with Him, that the body of sin might be destroyed, that henceforth we should not serve sin. 7 For he that is dead is freed from sin. 8 Now if we be dead with Christ, we believe that we shall also live with Him: 9 Knowing that Christ being raised from the dead dieth no more; death hath no more dominion over Him. 10 For in that he died, he died unto sin once: but in that he liveth, he liveth unto God. 11 Likewise reckon ye also yourselves to be dead indeed unto sin, but alive unto God through Jesus Christ our Lord. 12 Let not sin therefore reign in your mortal body, that ye should obey it in the lusts thereof. 13 Neither yield ye your members as instruments of unrighteousness unto sin: but yield yourselves unto God, as those that are alive from the dead, and your members as instruments of righteousness unto God. 14 For sin shall not have dominion over you: for ye are not under the law, but under grace.* We know what He did for us and we are free because of it. We remember that we are washed and redeemed and made righteous. We choose what we will allow ourselves to dwell on. We refuse to focus on the lies of the enemy. We stand upon the power in the blood and in the Word of God, and draw our strength and confidence from Christ alone.

"God recreated you, imparted to your spirit His own Nature. Now you stand before Him as though you had never been weak, as though you had never been a failure, as though you had never been under condemnation." (Kenyon, p. 200) With that knowledge you can stand confident in the very presence of God and know that you are accepted and free. God chose to live with us and in us and calls us to continually come closer to Him. "The highest honor He has ever conferred upon us is to be joint-fellowshippers with Himself, with His Son and with the Holy Spirit in carrying out His dream for the Redemption of the human race. Relationship without fellowship is an insipid, tasteless thing." (Kenyon, p. 218) God wants us near Him. He calls us to meet Him on the mountains of faith and fellowship. We climb with the same one who climbed Calvary. He desires our time and attention and He will do whatever is necessary to draw us to Himself.

Luke 6:12 *12 And it came to pass in those days, that he went out into a mountain to pray, and continued all night in prayer to God.*

# Jesus Went to the Mountain – Prayer

If Jesus who was perfect needed to pray, we certainly do. God has urged us to pray, but to many people prayer remains a mystery, or a difficult task. Prayer was always meant to be a conversation between God and His loved ones. It is a devout communion, and a joining in harmony with God. It is the place where we ask of Him, that is petition. It is where we cry out for others, that is intercession. It is also the place where we express our love and gratitude and come for forgiveness.

There should be no fear in approaching God. He is holy, but He is also your Father. God loves you and longs for time with you. He wants you to share the whole of your life with Him. He wants you to talk with Him. Jesus walked in perfect unity with the Father and He wants you to enjoy that same relationship.

In these few of the many references to Jesus praying, we can easily see that He lived a life of prayer. When Jesus heard that John the Baptist was killed He sought solitude in a quiet place to commune with God. He was followed and responded by ministering to the crowds. After preaching and healing the sick and feeding the 5000 He withdrew to a mountain to pray. **Matthew 14:23 (KJV)** *23 And when he had sent the multitudes away, he went up into a mountain apart to pray: and when the evening was come, he was there alone.* It was there in the presence of God that Jesus gained the strength and peace to continue to minister to the masses. He filled up so He could pour out His life to others. That is one reason why fellowship is so important for believers. We minister out of the supply in the spirit that we gain in the presence of God. Jesus understood the importance of drawing away to unite with the Father.

That was not the only time we see the Lord go to the mountain to pray. Before choosing His disciples Jesus went to meet His Father on the mountain. **Luke 6:12 (KJV)** *12 And it came to pass in those days, that he went out into a mountain to pray, and continued all night in prayer to God.* The Lord sought out a solitary place to seek His Father and the instructions that He needed. He did not voice a short utterance, or request. Jesus went and stayed in the presence of God all night long. He did not need to stay that long to get an answer, but He longed for fellowship and He immersed Himself in that glorious presence until life demanded that He leave. That is the same passion that should motivate His followers. Whenever Jesus had need, or sorrow or wanted companionship, He went to the mountain and prayed. One Old Testament statement that references that idea of going to a solitary place to seek the Lord is found in **Psalm 46:10 (KJV)** *10 Be still, and know that I am God…* Generally speaking we find it hard to draw away and just quiet ourselves before the Lord, but there is great peace and power in quietly drawing away. I think it is part of the reason my dad loved to fish. It was the stillness of the water and the quiet time there. I don't know if daddy prayed when he went fishing, but I often did.

The disciples saw what Jesus gained from time with the Father and they asked Jesus to help them to learn to live as He did. They wanted that life that was led by God. They wanted the confidence and compassion that was present in Jesus and they knew if they were to have what He had, they must dwell in the presence of the Most High. They had to know God, and that required that they develop a prayer life.

Jesus started by teaching them the basics. He assumed that men would converse with God. He did not say "If you pray." He said, "When you pray." **Matthew 6:5-8 (KJV)** *5 And when thou prayest, thou shalt not be as the hypocrites are: for they love to pray standing in the synagogues and in the corners of the streets, that they may be seen of men. Verily I say unto you, They have their reward. 6 But thou, when thou prayest, enter into thy closet, and when thou hast shut thy door, pray to thy Father which is in secret; and thy Father which seeth in secret shall reward thee openly.* Get away from the distractions and interruptions of life, because you are entering into the Lord's presence. You need to be conscious that you are approaching your Creator, the One who is worthy of more respect than any man on earth. Shut down all the junk that is going on in your life and listen. Humble yourself. Realize that God, Emanuel, is right there present with you. It makes prayer more vital and powerful and less of a chore when you recognize He has invited you to spend time alone with Him. *7 But when ye pray, use not vain repetitions, as the heathen do: for they think that they shall be heard for their much speaking. 8 Be not ye therefore like unto them: for your Father knoweth what things ye have need of, before ye ask Him.* Don't just say empty words over and over. Don't say anything you don't really mean. God knows what you need and He cares. He has had compassion on you from the beginning. You never have to beg or bargain with God. He wants to meet your needs and bless you. He wants that time with you more than you want it. God is passionate about His love for you and has committed Himself wholly to you.

Jesus would habitually draw away and spend time communing with His Father. He often went to the mountains to pray. The disciples knew that Jesus prayed freely and they sought to understand that prayer connection. There was a confidence and a fellowship that came from the time Jesus was with the Father. It was such a lifestyle that they wanted Him to teach them how to enter into that place of unity called prayer. Most people call this the Lord's prayer, it is more accurate to call it the disciples' prayer; it is a portrait of what they were taught to pray. **Luke 11:1-4 (KJV)** *1 And it came to pass, that, as he was praying in a certain place, when he ceased, one of His disciples said unto Him, Lord, teach us to pray, as John also taught his disciples. 2 And he said unto them, When ye pray, say, Our Father which art in heaven, Hallowed be thy name. Thy kingdom come. Thy will be done, as in heaven, so in earth. 3 Give us day by day our daily bread. 4 And forgive us our sins; for we also forgive every one that is indebted to us. And lead us not into temptation; but deliver us from evil. For thine is the kingdom, and the power, and the glory, for ever. Amen.*

He never said to repeat those exact words, but to use them as a pattern. Let's walk through them as recorded by Matthew. **Matthew 6:9-13 (KJV)** *9 After this manner therefore pray ye: Our Father which art in heaven, Hallowed be thy name.* Begin in worship. Honor God as your father because relationship is foundational. He is holy, and sovereign, but He is also Abba, your Daddy who loves you. You recognize and honor the binding covenant that is between you. You share a bond of love with Him, so cherish it, and take hold of it. Pour out your love in words of admiration and thanksgiving. *10 Thy kingdom come. Thy will be done in earth, as it is in heaven.* Recognize that it is His kingdom and His will that matter, and align yourself with His word and His will. Put His plans before your desires. That sounds like Jesus praying in the Garden of Gethsemane, *"Not my will but thine be done."* Jesus purchased your salvation by means of His enormous sacrifice rather than asking for what was easy or comfortable. God's will on earth as it is in heaven, creates a perfect peace within the believer. Is there need in heaven? No. Is there sickness or lack or sorrow or death? No of course not. His will is always better than mine and He sees from a much higher perspective than my tiny view of the world. My pastor always says "Think about the big picture." We are asking for God to make this place like heaven. We are asking to fit into His plans. If it were God's will for our prayers to go unanswered then we would not need to pray. Jesus wanted us to have a life of abundance and freedom here just like in heaven. The thing is we base our happiness on circumstance and God does not. My peace is not based on how I feel today, but on the whole of His purposes on earth related to my overall good. I can trust that while I may not see it today, God is working all things out for my good. He loves me, and He wants more for me than I can ask or think. God knows more about my tomorrow than I do, so my comfort in the moment is not as important as the outcome He has designated for me. *11 Give us this day our daily bread.* Ask for what you need, recognize that this day He will provide all you need and when you need more He will be accessible again. Just as He sent manna in the wilderness daily, you cannot expect an extended supply but you can expect today's supply. Also recognize that it is

He who sustains you. He called Himself the Bread of Life; when you pray for daily bread you also pray for more of Him. He will take care of your natural needs but the spirit of man is always more important than his body. Go to the bread of life and He will nourish you. **John 6:35 (KJV)** *35 And Jesus said unto them, I am the bread of life: he that cometh to me shall never hunger; and he that believeth on me shall never thirst.* Also **John 6:48-51 (KJV)** *48 I am that bread of life. 49 Your fathers did eat manna in the wilderness, and are dead. 50 This is the bread which cometh down from heaven, that a man may eat thereof, and not die. 51 I am the living bread which came down from heaven: if any man eat of this bread, he shall live forever: and the bread that I will give is my flesh, which I will give for the life of the world.* The true bread from heaven satisfies. Jesus who is the bread of life said to pray for daily bread. He said, "You can never survive a day without Me. Come seek Me and find Me, walk close to Me, and I will sustain you." Give us our daily bread covers all of our needs. Physical, financial, and spiritual needs are fully covered here, so all of you requests are in this portion. *12 And forgive us our debts, as we forgive our debtors.* He tied our own forgiveness with our attitude towards others. Always seek to please Him, maintain a spirit of repentance. Be quick to repent and quick to forgive others, your relationship with God and men is important and any bitterness or hatred will severely damage it. *13 And lead us not into temptation, but deliver us from evil:* Be alert to the snares of the devil and ask God to keep you out of them. Recognize that while it is not a sin to be tempted, it is a sin to give in to temptation. You can resist any and every temptation. **1 Corinthians 10:13 (KJV)** *13 There hath no temptation taken you but such as is common to man: but God is faithful, who will not suffer you to be tempted above that ye are able; but will with the temptation also make a way to escape, that ye may be able to bear it.* Ask for the

Lord's protection from the devil and all that is related to him. This is where you plead the blood. Mathew's version adds **Matthew 6:13 (KJV)** ... *For thine is the kingdom, and the power, and the glory, forever. Amen.* You acknowledge the sovereign God by coming full circle. Worship Him. Let your heart love on God. Spend considerable time meditating on how awesome and powerful and amazing God is. Think about how the Creator of heaven and earth is attune to your heart's cry. He is unfathomable, but He wants you to know Him. It is in worship that we comprehend what can be known of God. It is the time when we are most focused upon Him, and He is most free to reveal Himself to us. Jesus then came back to the idea of a clean, forgiving heart. **Matthew 6:14-15 (KJV)** *14 For if ye forgive men their trespasses, your heavenly Father will also forgive you: 15 But if ye forgive not men their trespasses, neither will your Father forgive your trespasses.* God linked our willingness to forgive to our access to His grace and mercy. He wants us to walk in perpetual unity and He does not want our prayers hindered. Every man had a sin debt, but Jesus paid it in full. Our own redemption makes us responsible to minister the same grace God poured out on us. We must be quick to forgive others freeing them from the depth of our hearts. We owe that compassion and mercy that we received to those who deserve it the least.

Now that we are saved it is up to us to stay free from the sin of the world. We are instructed to take every additional sin and failure and let the blood cleanse it. **1 John 1:9 (KJV)** *9 If we confess our sins, he is faithful and just to forgive us our sins, and to cleanse us from all unrighteousness.* We need forgiveness often, so we need to stay penitent, quick to turn away from all sin so He can cover it.

Jesus taught the disciples how to pray and then He added this illustration about persistent prayer. **Luke 11:1-8 (KJV)** *5 And he said unto them, Which of you shall have a friend, and shall go unto him at midnight, and say unto him, Friend, lend me three loaves;* Be specific, the man did not just ask for food for his visitor, he wanted three loaves. *6 For a friend of mine in his journey is come to me, and I have nothing to set before him? 7 And he from within shall answer and say, Trouble me not: the door is now shut, and my children are with me in bed; I cannot rise and give thee.* Our petitioner went at an inconvenient time, but because he had relationship with his neighbor he was confident to ask for provision. Then he kept asking until he got the help he needed. *8 I say unto you, Though he will not rise and give him, because he is his friend, yet because of his importunity he will rise and give him as many as he needeth.* Never lose faith and stop praying—be persistent. The man was his neighbor, which implied he was a friend, in the Bible that indicates covenant relationship. That man was someone who should have been willing to help. We know that our God is willing to help us in our time of need.

**Luke 11:9-10 (KJV)** *9 And I say unto you, Ask, and it shall be given you; seek, and ye shall find; knock, and it shall be opened unto you. 10 For every one that asketh receiveth; and he that seeketh findeth; and to Him that knocketh it shall be opened.* Ask and keep asking. Search and seek and look for Him with your whole heart and you will find Him. Knock at the door, be persistent, the man who will not be denied is almost never denied. Come to God often and when you come recognize that it is His will to bless you. Knowing His word will keep you from asking for what is against His will, and it will give you a foundation for your request.

If I was a little child and I recognized Jesus, I think I would have run to Him. He was surrounded by children. When mothers brought their babies to Him, Jesus prayed for them. Most of them probably did not need healing, but He was present and they just wanted Him near their little ones. The purest form of prayer is fellowship. It is good to come sometimes like a little child with no need, no request, just a heart that wants to be near the Lord.

When people were in need, they called upon Jesus and He prayed. He often touched the sick, and his touch brought healing. Martha and Mary called upon Him when their brother was seriously sick, they asked Him to come, but He delayed. Lazarus was dead for four days before Jesus arrived. When His friend Lazarus lay dead in the grave Jesus prayed in an unexpected manner. He was not filled with sorrow, but with expectant faith. He asked for permission to roll away the stone. He was about to exhume the body and speak resurrection life into it. He wanted Lazarus to be free to join Him. **John 11:41-43 (KJV)** *41 Then they took away the stone from the place where the dead was laid. And Jesus lifted up His eyes, and said, Father, I thank thee that thou hast heard me. 42 And I knew that thou hearest me always: but because of the people which stand by I said it, that they may believe that thou hast sent me.* That is all we know of the prayer, from there He just spoke with authority. When did the Father hear Jesus? He heard Him every time Jesus prayed before. God heard Him when Jesus said, *"This sickness shall not end in death."* The Father heard Him when Jesus said *"Lazarus is asleep, but I go to wake Him."* The Father heard Jesus when He told Martha and Mary that Lazarus would live again and that He was the resurrection and the Life. God heard every word Jesus spoke concerning His friend and all of His words lined up with the divine purpose of restoring life. *43 And when he thus* *had spoken, he cried with a loud voice, Lazarus, come forth.* Prayer was so natural to Jesus that He drifted in and out of it knowing that He had perpetual fellowship and access to the Father. That is what He wants for us. **Ephesians 6:18 (NIV)** *18 And pray in the Spirit on all occasions with all kinds of prayers and requests. With this in mind, be alert and always keep on praying for all the Lord's people.* Pray continually, pray passionately, follow the example of our Lord; climb to that quiet place in the mountains and pray.

The Scriptures also say this about prayer. **1 Thessalonians 5:16-22 (KJV)** *16 Rejoice evermore. 17 Pray without ceasing. 18 In every thing give thanks: for this is the will of God in Christ Jesus concerning you. 19 Quench not the Spirit. 20 Despise not prophesyings. 21 Prove all things; hold fast that which is good. 22 Abstain from all appearance of evil.* That is the attitude of prayer—having a thankful heart and a sensitive spirit and being instantly able to turn from your surroundings to the One who is Lord over all of it. Prayer was never intended to be a monologue, it is a dialogue—that is a two way conversation, speaking and then listening. If that is true, and it is, then God is willing to communicate with us constantly.

Jesus commanded His disciples to pray for others. Intercession is an important part of our prayer lives. **Matthew 5:44 (KJV)** *44 But I say unto you, Love your enemies, bless them that curse you, do good to them that hate you, and pray for them which despitefully use you, and persecute you;* He also said we needed to both watch and pray in order to be ready for His return. **Mark 13:33 (KJV)** *33 Take ye heed, watch and pray: for ye know not when the time is.* There is an urgency to build the kingdom so He told us to pray for the souls of others. We are to help build His kingdom. **Matthew 9:37-38 (KJV)** *37 Then saith he unto His disciples,*

*The harvest truly is plenteous, but the labourers are few; 38 Pray ye therefore the Lord of the harvest, that he will send forth labourers into His harvest.*

He has told us repeatedly to go to the Father for our needs and the needs of others. Jesus wanted us to seek God and His wisdom and instructions. He has made it clear He wants us to live a life connected to the Father and that connection is prayer.

Spend time alone with God, seek out that time in the mountains and daily find Him ready and willing to commune with you and then when the urgent time of need comes, there will be no barrier when you need to call upon Him.

Lamentations 3:22-25 (KJV) *22 It is of the LORD'S mercies that we are not consumed, because his compassions fail not. They are new every morning: great is thy faithfulness. . 23 They are new every morning: great is thy faithfulness. 24 The LORD is my portion, saith my soul; therefore will I hope in him. 225 The LORD is good unto them that wait for him, to the soul that seeketh him.*

## The Lord is my Portion

The Lord is my portion. He is my inheritance. It is God that I want and lay claim to. More than any possession or purpose or treasure, the heart of man wants to find and maintain a relationship with God. The reason Caleb could say give me that mountain is because deep down he trusted in God. His faith in God was more of an inheritance than the land itself. The land was his gift, but his faith was in the Giver. We know the Giver too. It is not the gift within His hand that we seek but God Himself.

God is mine. **Lamentations 3:21-25 (KJV)** *21 This I recall to my mind, therefore have I hope. 22 It is of the LORD'S mercies that we are not consumed, because His compassions fail not. 23 They are new every morning: great is thy faithfulness. 24 The LORD is my portion, saith my soul; therefore will I hope in Him. 25 The LORD is good unto them that wait for Him, to the soul that seeketh Him.* My portion of the inheritance is not silver or gold; it is real treasure. My portion is God's love.

Our relationship with God is not supposed to wear out or even wear thin. It is supposed to be renewed daily. His love and compassion are available at every moment. He will be our inheritance, our portion, but we must seek Him and depend on Him. The Lord is never slack in His efforts to touch us, but it is we who do not remember Him and turn our hearts toward Him. We are meant to climb to that place where we meet with the Lord daily.

The nature of the believer should be that of the bride who is truly in love with her groom. It is meant to be a loving journey, a daily living out of the awesome passion that caused Him to go to such lengths to purchase us—His bride. He has won our hearts but we can let the passion dwindle and become ordinary if we do not intentionally seek after Him. Remember how in Rev. 2:4 He said return to your first love. Fall in love with Jesus again. Come back into that place of intimacy. **Psalm 16:11 (KJV)** *11 Thou wilt shew me the path of life: in thy presence is fullness of joy; at thy right hand there are pleasures for evermore.*

**Psalm 16:5 (KJV)** *5 The LORD is the portion of mine inheritance and of my cup: thou maintainest my lot.* That part about Him being my cup is a cultural reference. We can see it more clearly in the 23rd Psalm. **Psalm 23:5 (KJV)** *5 Thou preparest a table before me in the presence of mine enemies: thou anointest my head with oil; my cup runneth over.* The Lord sets me down to feast with Him at His table. The entire world sees it. My Lord blesses me in front of the ones who dishonor me. He anoints me with the oil of gladness and the precious Holy Spirit. The part I really wanted to focus on is this last portion of the verse about my cup running over. In many eastern cultures it was a sign of welcome for the host to pour wine into your cup. If you were welcome to stay your cup never went totally dry. If it was time for you to leave, a dry cup was a hint to go home. If you ignored the hint your cup was turned over, which was very embarrassing. If however the wealthy king who was hosting this party was in love with you, he would pour into your cup until the cup could not contain the drink. The wine spilling over onto the ground as he continued to pour was a sign of deep love. That was a proposal of marriage. He was saying stay with me always. When God called us to be the bride of Christ, we could join the Psalmist in saying, "My cup runneth over." God wants us with Him always. He covets time with us. He cherishes the moments of intimacy that we share with Him.

The psalmist claims relationship again in chapter 119 and 142. **Psalm 119:57-60 (KJV)** *57 Thou art my portion, O LORD: I have said that I would keep thy words. 58 I intreated thy favour with my whole heart: be merciful unto me according to thy word. 59 I thought on my ways, and turned my feet unto thy testimonies. 60 I made haste, and delayed not to keep thy commandments.* **Psalm 142:5 (KJV)** *5 I cried unto thee, O LORD: I said, Thou art my refuge and my portion in the land of the living.*

**Jeremiah 10:16 (KJV)** *16 The portion of Jacob is not like them: God who is the inheritance of Israel is not like any idol, or any manmade thing. For he is the former of all things; and Israel is the rod of his inheritance: The LORD of hosts is his name.* This is repeated word for word in Jeremiah 51:19.

If He is what I have and hold to and treasure, then I need to remember that I am His as well. **Song of Songs 6:3 (KJV)** *3 I am my beloved's, and my beloved is mine...* Look what it says about us belonging to God in the Old Testament. **Deuteronomy 32:8-9 (KJV)** *8 When the most High divided to the nations their inheritance, when he separated the sons of Adam, he set the bounds of the people according to the number of the children of Israel. 9 <u>For the LORD'S portion</u>*

*is his people; Jacob is the lot of his inheritance.* While this speaks of Israel in the Old Testament, all who will respond to His invitation become part of God's chosen people, the bride of Christ, and His inheritance in the New Testament.

Jesus prayed for His disciples and we as modern day disciples are part of that group. It is a picture of divine intimacy. **John 17:9-26 (KJV)** *9 I pray for them: I pray not for the world, but for them which thou hast given me; for they are thine.* We are His portion, and He is ours. The Father and Son share union with the ones they love. *10 And all mine are thine, and thine are mine; and I am glorified in them. 11 And now I am no more in the world, but these are in the world, and I come to thee. Holy Father, keep through thine own name those whom thou hast given me, that they may be one, as we are.* Jesus was pleading our case, crying out for us to have oneness with the whole of the Trinity. *12 While I was with them in the world, I kept them in thy name: those that thou gavest me I have kept, and none of them is lost, but the son of perdition; that the Scripture might be fulfilled.* Jesus loved His disciples, including Judas, and including you. He said I have maintained relationship with all of them except Judas who chose to walk away. *13 And now come I to thee; and these things I speak in the world, that they might have my joy fulfilled in themselves. 14 I have given them thy word; and the world hath hated them, because they are not of the world, even as I am not of the world. 15 I pray not that thou shouldest take them out of the world, but that thou shouldest keep them from the evil. 16 They are not of the world, even as I am not of the world. 17 Sanctify them through thy truth: thy word is truth. 18 As thou hast sent me into the world, even so have I also sent them into the world. 19 And for their sakes I sanctify myself, that they also might be sanctified through the truth.* Jesus is praying specifically for us born again Christians from here on. *20*

*Neither pray I for these alone, but for them also which shall believe on me through their word; 21 That they all may be one; as thou, Father, art in me, and I in thee, that they also may be one in us: that the world may believe that thou hast sent me. 22 And the glory which thou gavest me I have given them; that they may be one, even as we are one: 23 I in them, and thou in me, that they may be made perfect in one; and that the world may know that thou hast sent me, and hast loved them, as thou hast loved me. 24 Father, I will that they also, whom thou hast given me, be with me where I am; that they may behold my glory, which thou hast given me: for thou lovedst me before the foundation of the world. 25 O righteous Father, the world hath not known thee: but I have known thee, and these have known that thou hast sent me. 26 And I have declared unto them thy name, and will declare it: that the love wherewith thou hast loved me may be in them, and I in them.*

God is seeking for individual time with His own children. He wants you. He does not want your money or your talent or your effort, all He really wants is your heart. He wants your whole heart. He is calling to you again, come meet me on the mountain, come away with me. **Matthew 7:7 (KJV)** *7 Ask, and it shall be given you; seek, and ye shall find; knock, and it shall be opened unto you.* Do you really think that is about getting your need met? It is more than that. Ask for more of Him, seek more of Him, and be persistent. Keep climbing until you find that place in His presence. Never let what is precious like the truth of the gospel and the power of the Spirit and the beauty of your relationship become devalued in your life. It is a great treasure.

David understood that treasure. **Psalm 84:2 (KJV)** *2 My soul longeth, yea, even fainteth for the courts of the LORD: my heart and my flesh crieth out for the living*

*God.* He who hungers after God will be satisfied in God's presence. God valued that desire in David so highly that He called David, *"A man after my own heart."*

The true author of the Bible is the Holy Spirit, who inspired and directed men to pen His words. He says there is a renewing and refreshing that comes from our time with Him. **Acts 3:19 (KJV) 19** *Repent ye therefore, and be converted, that your sins may be blotted out, when the times of refreshing shall come from the presence of the Lord;* There is a refreshing, reviving presence and we want that. The times of refreshing come from time spent with Him, one on one. That word refreshing means the restoration of breath. That sounds like a lifesaving measure being given to a dying man, it sounds like spiritual CPR. Think about it. The very breath of God, the Holy Spirit, will breathe into men when they are in His presence. That is why we have revivals and conferences to get a concentration of His presence and draw near. Peter was telling them to draw near with expectation of revelation. He said this right after a great miracle. He wanted them to know more than just an expression of the presence; He wanted them to know the One who was the miracle worker. Peter was trying to reveal truth about the One who loved us so much He would take on our life and death and give us His very nature—His life. He wanted their relationship to be personal and full. He wanted them to see the importance of a personal walk with God. He wanted them to know the joy of union with the Lord who is their inheritance, and their portion. You are God's beloved, His inheritance, His portion and God is yours.

## Ascending Praise & Worship

Praise and honor and worship are the pathway up the mountain of God into His presence. **Psalm 99:9 (KJV)** *9 Exalt the LORD our God, and worship at His holy hill; for the LORD our God is holy.* We come to God with no offering of our own except the words on our lips and the love in our hearts. We rejoice in the small imperfect vision we have of our Lord. We can see from Scripture that great men and women of faith in the past knew the importance of honoring the Lord as they tried to draw near.

We can hear the ascension into God's presence in the words of the Psalmist. **Psalm 103:1-5 (KJV)** *1 Bless the LORD, O my soul: and all that is within me, bless His holy name. 2 Bless the LORD, O my soul, and forget not all His benefits: 3 Who forgiveth all thine iniquities; who healeth all thy diseases; 4 Who redeemeth thy life from destruction; who crowneth thee with lovingkindness and tender mercies; 5 Who satisfieth thy mouth with good things; so that thy youth is renewed like the eagle's.* Let all that I am recognize and glorify all that God is and all that He does.

**Psalm 104:1 (KJV)** *1 Bless the LORD, O my soul. O LORD my God, thou art very great; thou art clothed with honour and majesty.* It is the privilege and the duty of man to seek to honor and glorify God. We come to Him who is sovereign and powerful, and go beyond our words and actions to the place where worship begins. Real praise and worship stems from the heart of man. What little we understand about Him draws us towards Him. It becomes our deepest desire to know Him more fully. Our love for the Lord grows stronger with each encounter. There is a divine romance between God and man.

**Psalm 100:4 (KJV)** *4 Enter into His gates with thanksgiving, and into His courts with praise: be thankful unto Him, and bless His name.* If we want the presence of God this is a good place to begin the journey. We come recognizing His goodness and holiness and we honor Him above all others. The terms for entry and for access into His presence are thanksgiving and praise. We understand both of them. We come with a grateful heart and we praise Him, rejoice over Him. "Thanksgiving relates to God's goodness. Praise relates to God's greatness but Worship relates to God's holiness. Holiness is in a class by itself. It is the attribute of God that is most difficult for the human mind to comprehend because it has no parallel on earth." (Prince, p. 16) "He is like no other and none compare to the wonder of Him…He is so much more wonderful than anything—even His blessings." (Bevere, p. 4)

David understood some things about praise and worship. David who had the honor of men, understood about a quality decision to honor and worship God. As King, David understood positions of authority and that helped him to respond as he recognized the God above all others. We can never come to God without understanding how great and awesome He is. David chose to honor the Lord and we must choose it too. **Psalm 5:7 (KJV)** *7 But as for me, I will come into thy house in the multitude of thy mercy: and in thy fear will I worship toward thy holy temple.* When we enter into real worship there is reverence and then communion with Him and that is the place where revelation comes. There is no place of fellowship outside of recognition of God's immense greatness and holiness.

**Psalm 22:3 (KJV)** *3 But thou art holy, O thou that inhabitest the praises of Israel.* He abides in, and lives surrounded by the praise of His people. Where there is no praise, you will not find an ongoing manifested presence of God. **Psalm 108:1-5 (KJV)** *1 O God, my heart is fixed; I will sing and give praise, even with my glory. 2 Awake, psaltery and harp: I myself will awake early. 3 I will praise thee, O LORD, among the people: and I will sing praises unto thee among the nations. 4 For thy mercy is great above the heavens: and thy truth reacheth unto the clouds. 5 Be thou exalted, O God, above the heavens: and thy glory above all the earth;* The writer established a connection by continually walking in honor of God.

**Psalm 96:9 (KJV)** *9 O worship the LORD in the beauty of holiness: fear before Him, all the earth.* There are very few places where people reverence God that way today, and only a few places where anointed praise and worship are really offered to God. Much of what happens in church "worship services" is more entertainment for the congregation than enticing an audience of one. We worship the One true God. Jesus said that *"Those who worship God must worship Him in Spirit and truth."* [See John 4:21-24] That means we come sincerely and with purity and a deep longing to please God. We come without deception or pretense. We also come in surrender to the Holy Spirit. We come as a triune being, Spirit, soul and body. Each part of man is yielded with differing responsibilities and actions, the whole of man comes, clean, and committed in heart and mind. The fullness of the man must be present for our worship to be acceptable. Worship must stem from more than the mind of man—true worship is a spirit inspired response to the Lord we love.

There is an ascendency into the presence of God that is more than words of praise. Worship is deeper it is related to and focused on the holiness of God. We have no earthly frame of reference for holiness. I sang a solo at church once that sums up my sense of inadequacy at declaring His holiness. The lyrics include, "What do I know of Holy?" and "I think I made you too small, I never knew you at all." My favorite line says, "The slightest hint of you brought me down to my knees." [Addison Road, "What do I know of Holy."] What indeed do I know of holy? It is the single descriptive concept of the One who is so beyond my intellect and experience.

Our definition is weak because we can only see it from our viewpoint. God is to be hallowed or worshiped because He is holy and there is nothing holy in that sense here on earth. We can try to understand by using the Strong's Hebrew word H6942 **qadosh** meaning sacred, ceremonially and morally pure, the Holy One who is God. The Greek word is **hagios** G40 and means essentially the same thing with the added aspect of being "awful" in my opinion more overwhelming and intimidating. It is still beyond our grasp. To worship is to bow down and humble ourselves before Him. It is a deep loving attitude of the heart, more than words we speak or songs we sing. Worship is almost entirely a submission to and acknowledgment of Him as other than human. It resembles the overwhelming smallness we feel when we first stand on the shore and see the oceans, knowing He poured them from the palm of His hand. Worship celebrates God being higher, mightier and so much more than man. Worship consists of baring our souls before the Creator and the Lover of mankind. It is intimate and personal.

**1 Timothy 1:17 (KJV) 17** *Now unto the King eternal, immortal, invisible, the only wise God, be honour and glory for ever and ever. Amen.* That is an effort at worship. While I may not define it clearly, I know real worship when I enter into it. Earthly worship is similar to that which is offered continually in heaven. We have both Old Testament and New Testament examples from those who caught a glimpse into the spirit realm.

**Isaiah 6:1-4 (KJV)** *1 In the year that king Uzziah died I saw also the Lord sitting upon a throne, high and lifted up, and His train filled the temple. 2 Above it stood the seraphims: each one had six wings; with twain he covered His face, and with twain he covered His feet, and with twain he did fly. 3 And one cried unto another, and said, Holy, holy, holy, is the LORD of hosts: the whole earth is full of His glory. 4 And the posts of the door moved at the voice of Him that cried, and the house was filled with smoke.* Holy, Holy, Holy is the cry of the angels here it is the same scene recorded by John in the New Testament. **Revelation 4:8-11 (KJV)** *8 And the four beasts had each of them six wings about him; and they were full of eyes within: and they rest not day and night, saying,* <u>*Holy, holy, holy, Lord God Almighty, which was, and is, and is to come.*</u> *9 And when those beasts give glory and honour and thanks to him that sat on the throne, who liveth for ever and ever, 10 The four and twenty elders* *fall down before him that sat on the throne, and worship him that liveth for ever and ever, and cast their crowns before the throne, saying, 11 Thou art worthy, O Lord, to receive glory and honour and power: for thou hast created all things, and for thy pleasure they are and were created.* That is true worship. They bow down, humbling themselves. Their words and actions display their reverence and they cry out Holy. "I believe there is significance in the threefold repetition. I think holy is the Father; holy is the Son; holy is the Spirit. And no one else is holy. God is unique in His holiness. And we can only understand or become partakers of holiness insofar as we relate to God." (Prince, p. 29) There is an infinite realm to the glory of God. In some ways I like to think that the angels cry out night and day because with every glimpse of God they see another aspect of His glory. They cannot help but to cry out holy with each new revelation of holiness. The angels called attention to the fact that God is eternal; they used all the markers for time to show God is forever present in all of history and both before and after. I believe they referenced and honored the Lord's resurrection. I think the throwing down of their crowns is an effort to say that whatever any of us accomplishes is just another of His gifts and we restore the honor anyone gave us by laying it at His feet. They called Him a benevolent Creator. Finally, it says here they never stop saying how wonderful and awesome and powerful God is, day and night for all of eternity. Worship has to become a lifestyle.

I am His and He is mine. There is unity with God—it is a love story that the Word of God has recorded. God sought us out, gave a king's ransom and more for us. He pulled us out of slavery. Jesus ransomed and redeemed us at the cost of divine blood and brought us unto Himself. He says, "This one is mine." And our hearts cry out for the Lover of our souls.

**Hebrews 12:28 (KJV)** *28 Wherefore we receiving a kingdom which cannot be moved, let us have grace, whereby we may serve God acceptably with reverence and godly fear:* Worship establishes us as belonging to God. "One of the essential things about worship is focusing on the Lord, turning away from ourselves—as it were almost merging our identity with His." (Prince, p. 36) I love the intimacy of that, His soul merged with mine. My heart entwined with His—that is the deepest desire from the very center of my being. **Revelation 7:12 (KJV)** *12 Saying, Amen: Blessing, and glory, and wisdom, and thanksgiving, and honour, and power, and might, be unto our God for ever and ever. Amen.* He who is worthy of all of those attributes and more is my Lord and I cry out to Him with love and admiration, "You are holy." That is an attempt at worship. I fall down like the angels and my tears speak what words fail to say. That too is an attempt to worship and honor Him. As I approach the mountain of the Lord, I tremble but I continue to ascend because to worship and honor and praise Him is to draw nearer to Him and the whole of my heart cries out for more of God. With great joy, I climb knowing that He longs for my presence too.

1 Kings 19:12 ... *and after the fire a still small voice.*

John 10:27 *My sheep hear my voice, and I know them, and they follow me:*

# From Mt. Carmel to Mt. Horeb

    Men of God have always spoken to the masses for Him. Elijah was one such prophet who declared the Word of the Lord with power and authority. It was not without cost, that he was God's minister. It will not be effortless and painless for any of us to walk as Elijah did. First God declared a drought. This was punishment for all who had entered into Baal worship. Their false religion led Israel to bow down to an idol that "controlled the storms." Baal was supposed to send them rain. The prophet said there will be no rain until I say so, and I won't speak it until God says to. Elijah like everyone else had to deal with the dry conditions. At God's command he drank from a brook and ate what ravens brought him. After a time the brook dried up, and Elijah got new instruction for his provisions. Eventually, he was sent to depend upon a widow to lodge him and God to sustain him and his hosts. In the third year of the drought,

God calls him to reveal himself to King Ahab. Ahab wants him dead. Those three long years were a time of judgment against Baal; the drought should have turned people away from Baal worship but instead they grew more deeply imbedded into it. It was then that God sent Elijah to Mt. Carmel, a place where both the worship of the Lord had been practiced and now Baal worship flourished.

The Hebrew people had grown cold and indifferent and had incorporated the worship of several so called "gods" into their daily lives. In short, they had made light of their covenant relationship. They acted as if God was no longer powerful, almost as if He was no different from the idols around them. God would not allow them to stay in that compromised state. His prophet, Elijah, called the people together and asked them to make a commitment to follow God completely or sever their ties to the Lord and worship idols. Victory on Mt. Carmel would decide who was really LORD in Israel. Elijah opposed the 450 prophets of Baal in a contest for the loyalty of the people. It was a winner take all gamble and there was no doubt in the mind of Elijah that God would indeed be proven to be supreme.

**1 Kings 18:21-25 (KJV)** *21 And Elijah came unto all the people, and said, How long halt ye between two opinions? If the LORD be God, follow Him: but if Baal, then follow him. And the people answered him not a word. 22 Then said Elijah unto the people, I, even I only, remain a prophet of the LORD; but Baal's prophets are four hundred and fifty men. 23 Let them therefore give us two bullocks; and let them choose one bullock for themselves, and cut it in pieces, and lay it on wood, and put no fire under: and I will dress the other bullock, and lay it on wood, and put no fire under: 24 And call ye on the name of your gods, and I will call on the name of the LORD: and the God that answereth by fire, let him be God. And all the people answered and* *said, It is well spoken.* In the face of great opposition this man of faith said what he believed to be truth based on his relationship with the God of Israel. The people agreed to his terms. *25 And Elijah said unto the prophets of Baal, Choose you one bullock for yourselves, and dress it first; for ye are many; and call on the name of your gods, but put no fire under.* They did everything they knew to get a response from the false god they served. Those 450 men cried out, and made foolish gestures and even spilled their own blood next to their sacrifice, but there was no answer. All their worldly attempts to bring about a manifestation fell flat. Absolutely nothing happened. It was not enough for Baal to be disgraced and shown to be weak; the LORD must be proven strong. So Elijah offered his sacrifice to the Lord who would answer so clearly the people could not miss it.

**1 Kings 18:30-35 (KJV)** *30 And Elijah said unto all the people, Come near unto me. And all the people came near unto him. And he repaired the altar of the LORD that was broken down.* Elijah knew he was calling upon the same God who had entered into covenant with Abraham and Isaac and Jacob. *31 And Elijah took twelve stones, according to the number of the tribes of the sons of Jacob, unto whom the word of the LORD came, saying, Israel shall be thy name: 32 And with the stones he built an altar in the name of the LORD: and he made a trench about the altar, as great as would contain two measures of seed. 33 And he put the wood in order, and cut the bullock in pieces, and laid him on the wood, And said, Fill four barrels with water, and pour it on the burnt sacrifice, and on the wood. 34 And he said, Do it the second time. And they did it the second time. And he said, Do it the third time. And they did it the third time. 35 And the water ran round about the altar; and he filled the trench also with water.* The prophet was not afraid to put God to the test. That was twelve barrels full of water, but

Elijah was following instructions. Faith and presumption are two entirely different things. He did not act on his own, but he responded with obedience to the only One who could prove His lordship. Everything was soaked and there was a moat surrounding the altar. Elijah knew the God he served was more than able to answer with fire.

**1 Kings 18:36 – 39 (KJV)** *36And it came to pass at the time of the offering of the evening sacrifice, that Elijah the prophet came near, and said, LORD God of Abraham, Isaac, and of Israel, let it be known this day that thou art God in Israel, and that I am thy servant, and that I have done all these things at thy word.* He asked for the glory. It was not a long prayer; there was no worship music or any other religious activity. He simply called upon the Lord and the Lord answered him. *37Hear me, O LORD, hear me, that this people may know that thou art the LORD God, and that thou hast turned their heart back again. 38Then the fire of the LORD fell, and consumed the burnt sacrifice, and the wood, and the stones, and the dust, and licked up the water that was in the trench.* The fire answered the blood and the cry of a man who believed in the power of the covenant. That heavenly fire destroyed every remnant of what had been the altar. Stone and dirt and all the water in that trench were consumed by the flame. There was nothing left but a scorched plot of ground. *39And when all the people saw it, they fell on their faces: and they said, The LORD, he is the God; the LORD, he is the God.*

Elijah met with God on the mountain and the resulting fire that fell was proof that God was present. The doubting, double-minded people were now confident that God was real and powerful and present and it turned them back toward Him. God met with them in the place of their failure and unbelief and even the place where they had sinned. If He would do that for them, He will do it for us. God is willing to do whatever it takes to bring man back into fellowship.

Elijah proved the Lord was God by calling down fire from heaven. Then he killed the 450 false prophets. Once Baal could not get credit for it, Elijah prayed down rain. A cloud the size of a man's hand becomes a gully washer. He runs down the whole mountain and arrives before the horses and chariot of Ahab. It is just one miracle after another here. Elijah has seen and walked in great victory. Then one evil woman said she was going to kill him and Elijah runs away. He retreated into the wilderness about 28 miles and sat down in a fit of exhaustion and depression he says, "I am done, let me just die—I give up." That happens to us when we fight long and hard and it feels like we have been working alone and doing all we could. There is great victory followed by a word of discouragement and we just crumble under the pressure. We want to lie down weary and worn and frazzled. Do not forget that God sees the struggle, the faithfulness and the weariness.

Elijah was not the only spiritual leader to feel like giving up. Look at the frustration of Moses. **Numbers 11:11-15 (KJV)** *11 And Moses said unto the LORD, Wherefore hast thou afflicted thy servant? and wherefore have I not found favour in thy sight, that thou layest the burden of all this people upon me? 12 Have I conceived all this people? have I begotten them, that thou shouldest say unto me, Carry them in thy bosom, as a nursing father beareth the sucking child, unto the land which thou swarest unto their fathers? 13 Whence should I have flesh to give unto all this people? for they weep unto me, saying, Give us flesh, that we may eat. 14 I am not able to bear all this people alone, because it is too heavy for me. 15 And if thou deal thus with me, kill me, I pray thee, out of hand, if I have found favour in thy* *sight; and let me not see my wretchedness.* That sounds like the same frustrated, weary, overwhelmed attitude we saw in Elijah. God sent Moses help in the form of some assistant workers. He sent Elijah an angel to minister to him.

The Lord prescribed food and rest. He did not deal with Elijah immediately, but instead sent an angel who encouraged him and fed him between naps. Elijah went in the strength of what God gave him for forty days. It sustained the prophet when he was already weary and discouraged and got him to Mt. Horeb about 175 miles away. It was there that the Lord appeared to him again. He had called Elijah to another mountain to reveal Himself afresh. **1 Kings 19:11-18 (KJV)** *11 And he said, Go forth, and stand upon the mount before the LORD. And, behold, the LORD passed by, and a great and strong wind rent the mountains, and brake in pieces the rocks before the LORD; but the LORD was not in the wind: and after the wind an earthquake; but the LORD was not in the earthquake:* Those were powerful manifestations, they were spectacular, they were supernatural, but they were just flashes, not the true presence of God. Elijah was not seeking another experience. He needed time with the Lord. *12 And after the earthquake a fire; but the LORD was not in the fire:* God had been in the fire on Mt. Carmel but not this time. It was a strong shaking and a flame but it was still not God, so it was not enough to move Elijah. *and after the fire a still small voice.* The original language says it was just a breath of a whisper. God rarely shouts to us; He speaks tenderly and quietly, and in order to hear Him we must be still and listen intentionally. *13 And it was so, when Elijah heard it, that he wrapped His face in His mantle, and went out, and stood in the entering in of the cave. And, behold, there came a voice unto him, and said, What doest thou here, Elijah? 14 And he said, I have been very jealous for the LORD God of hosts: because the children of Israel have forsaken thy* *covenant, thrown down thine altars, and slain thy prophets with the sword; and I, even I only, am left; and they seek my life, to take it away...* God corrected Elijah, and told him that there were still faithful men and women who served the Lord. *18 Yet I have left me seven thousand in Israel, all the knees which have not bowed unto Baal, and every mouth which hath not kissed him.* Elijah responded to the whisper soft voice of God, because he knew that voice. In the New Testament Jesus tells us we can be assured we will know His voice too. **John 10:4 (KJV)** *4 And when he putteth forth his own sheep, he goeth before them, and the sheep follow Him: for they know His voice.* He said it again a few chapters later. **John 10:27 (KJV)** *27 My sheep hear my voice, and I know them, and they follow me:* Like Elijah, we do know the voice of God. We won't be fooled by another.

God met with Elijah and refreshed him and that time of fellowship on the mountain gave him all the strength and instructions he needed to finish strong. God knew that the discouraged heart of Elijah needed to know he was not alone in service to God. We know that there will always be a faithful few, a remnant that will believe and follow. Maybe like Elijah we feel alone, but God has an exact count of the faithful believers. Actually according to Malachi God has a written record of His own people. **Malachi 3:16-18 (KJV)** *16 Then they that feared the LORD spake often one to another: and the LORD hearkened, and heard it, and a book of remembrance was written before Him for them that feared the LORD, and that thought upon His name. 17 And they shall be mine, saith the LORD of hosts, in that day when I make up my jewels; and I will spare them, as a man spareth his own son that serveth him. 18 Then shall ye return, and discern between the righteous and the wicked, between him that serveth God and him that serveth him not.* I hope my name is in that book.

**2 Timothy 2:19 (KJV)** *19 Nevertheless the foundation of God standeth sure, having this seal, The Lord knoweth them that are His. And, Let every one that nameth the name of Christ depart from iniquity.* The One who loves us, knows us, and we know Him. We recognize His voice and come closer at the whisper of our name.

## Mt. Sinai

Mount Sinai is the location of one of the most dramatic and powerful manifestations of the Lord's presence. It was at Mount Sinai that the Ten Commandments were given and the base of the mountain is where the covenant was ratified. It is a place of meeting with the Lord and establishing the rules for living peacefully together in honor of the One True God. **Exodus 19:1 (KJV)** *1 In the third month, when the children of Israel were gone forth out of the land of Egypt, the same day came they into the wilderness of Sinai.* God was willing to meet with these His covenant people, but they must heed to His instructions, which they vowed to do. **Exodus 19:4-8 (KJV)** *4 Ye have seen what I did unto the Egyptians, and how I bare you on eagles' wings, and brought you unto myself. 5 Now therefore, if ye will obey my voice indeed, and keep my covenant, then ye shall be a peculiar treasure unto me above all people: for all the earth is mine: 6 And ye shall be unto me a kingdom of priests, and an holy nation. These are the words which thou shalt speak unto the children of Israel. 7 And Moses came and called for the elders of the people, and laid before their faces all these words which the LORD commanded him. 8 And all* *the people answered together, and said, All that the LORD hath spoken we will do. And Moses returned the words of the people unto the LORD.*

The children of Israel had seen the parting of the Red Sea. They had seen the pillar of fire and eaten food that fell from heaven. All those manifestations were powerful evidence that God was with them. Here at Mt. Sinai they would see and hear more directly from the Lord their God. **Exodus 19:9 (KJV)** *9 And the LORD said unto Moses, Lo, I come unto thee in a thick cloud, that the people may hear when I speak with thee, and believe thee forever. And Moses told the words of the people unto the LORD.*

**Exodus 19:16-24 (KJV)** *16 And it came to pass on the third day in the morning, that there were thunders and lightnings, and a thick cloud upon the mount, and the voice of the trumpet exceeding loud; so that all the people that was in the camp trembled. 17 And Moses brought forth the people out of the camp to meet with God; and they stood at the nether part of the mount. 18 And mount Sinai was altogether on a smoke, because the LORD descended upon it in fire: and the smoke thereof ascended as the smoke of a furnace, and the whole mount quaked greatly. 19 And when the voice of the trumpet sounded long, and waxed louder and louder, Moses spake, and God answered him by a voice.* The presence of God was awful, terrifying, and powerful; it resembled a volcanic eruption. There was lightning and thunder and fire and smoke and a host of overwhelming sights and sounds that the people feared. *20 And the LORD came down upon mount Sinai, on the top of the mount: and the LORD called Moses up to the top of the mount; and Moses went up. 21 And the LORD said unto Moses, Go down, charge the people, lest they break through unto the LORD to gaze, and many of them* *perish. 22 And let the priests also, which come near to the LORD, sanctify themselves, lest the LORD break forth upon them. 23 And Moses said unto the LORD, The people cannot come up to mount Sinai: for thou chargedst us, saying, Set bounds about the mount, and sanctify it. 24 And the LORD said unto him, Away, get thee down, and thou shalt come up, thou, and Aaron with thee: but let not the priests and the people break through to come up unto the LORD, lest he break forth upon them.* God was calling His own to climb higher and see more of Him in His glory.

**Exodus 20:18-21 (KJV)** *18 And all the people saw the thunderings, and the lightnings, and the noise of the trumpet, and the mountain smoking: and when the people saw it, they removed, and stood afar off. 19 And they said unto Moses, Speak thou with us, and we will hear: but let not God speak with us, lest we die.* There was a different nature in Moses. When all of the people saw and heard the manifested presence of God it caused them to flee, to cringe in fear. Moses was only inspired to draw even nearer. Any taste of the Lord's presence was enough to make him want to go higher, deeper into the things of God. It is always like that when God shows up. No one remains neutral. Either the hunger for more kicks in and we draw nearer at any cost and any effort or we turn aside. *20 And Moses said unto the people, Fear not: for God is come to prove you, and that his fear may be before your faces, that ye sin not. 21 And the people stood afar off, and Moses drew near unto the thick darkness where God was.*

**Exodus 24:3-8 (KJV)** *3 And Moses came and told the people all the words of the LORD, and all the judgments: and all the people answered with one voice, and said, All the words which the LORD hath said will we do. 4 And Moses wrote all the words of the LORD, and rose up early in the* *morning, and builded an altar under the hill, and twelve pillars, according to the twelve tribes of Israel. 5 And he sent young men of the children of Israel, which offered burnt offerings, and sacrificed peace offerings of oxen unto the LORD. 6 And Moses took half of the blood, and put it in basons; and half of the blood he sprinkled on the altar. 7 And he took the book of the covenant, and read in the audience of the people: and they said, All that the LORD hath said will we do, and be obedient. 8 And Moses took the blood, and sprinkled it on the people, and said, Behold the blood of the covenant, which the LORD hath made with you concerning all these words.* He established the covenant between the people and their God.

**Exodus 24:9-10 (KJV)** *9 Then went up Moses, and Aaron, Nadab, and Abihu, and seventy of the elders of Israel: 10 And they saw the God of Israel: and there was under His feet as it were a paved work of a sapphire stone, and as it were the body of heaven in his clearness.* Notice that these few from among the millions did get to see God. It says they saw at least His feet. It says that God stood on sapphire stone. I once heard Perry Stone teach that the common stone in Israel contained the right elements to create sapphires. The stone that was there in the mountain was changed by the fire of God's manifested presence and the corresponding heat turned it into sapphire. It would be similar to the process of heat and pressure that changes common coal into a diamond. If indeed God is the consuming fire that Scripture says He is, that would make perfect sense. Rev. Stone also believed that the tablets of stone, which were cut from the same mountain, also became sapphire because they were engraved by the hand of God.

**Exodus 24:13-18 (KJV)** *13 And Moses rose up, and His minister Joshua: and Moses went up into the mount of*

*God. 14 And he said unto the elders, Tarry ye here for us, until we come again unto you: and, behold, Aaron and Hur are with you: if any man have any matters to do, let him come unto them. 15 And Moses went up into the mount, and a cloud covered the mount. 16 And the glory of the LORD abode upon mount Sinai, and the cloud covered it six days: and the seventh day he called unto Moses out of the midst of the cloud. 17 And the sight of the glory of the LORD was like devouring fire on the top of the mount in the eyes of the children of Israel. 18 And Moses went into the midst of the cloud, and gat him up into the mount: and Moses was in the mount forty days and forty nights.*

God gave them the Law with the Ten Commandments and detailed instructions. While He was still speaking to Moses on the Mount, they rebelled and made an idol. As stated earlier, there are two distinct reactions to the presence of the Lord; people either want more of God or they are afraid. They either draw nearer or they retreat. When they got to Mount Sinai the people said we don't want to be so close, Moses you go and we will do what you tell us God said. The one man who wanted to draw near was allowed to draw near. We must be that one. The masses could not draw near because they were consumed by fear or maybe they had guilty consciences. Their souls were stained by their self-seeking ways. When we know we are made righteous by the blood of the Lamb, and we are walking in obedience to the word we already know, there is nothing that can hold us back from seeking more of the Lord and His presence.

We just want the One who made the mountain and who has manifested His presence there. We seek out that high place with God. We want the experience of men like Moses who had already been in the glory of His presence but kept asking for more of God. That attitude does not frustrate

God; it pleases Him. If we, like Moses, will hunger and thirst after the Lord, He will satisfy our longing.

**Exodus 33:12-23 (KJV)** *12 And Moses said unto the LORD, See, thou sayest unto me, Bring up this people: and thou hast not let me know whom thou wilt send with me. Yet thou hast said, I know thee by name, and thou hast also found grace in my sight. 13 Now therefore, I pray thee, if I have found grace in thy sight, shew me now thy way, that I may know thee, that I may find grace in thy sight: and consider that this nation is thy people.* Help me to understand you God, show me who you are, and let me understand your ways. I want to know you! That word "know" in the original Hebrew is Strong's word **#3045 yada** and it means to see, acknowledge, observe, comprehend, consider, discover and be endued with. It also includes to become a familiar friend, a kinsman, and to fully understand. It is the same exact word that we see in Genesis 4:1 Where Adam knew Eve and she conceived a son. Moses wants more of God and he has found the way obtain it. He says show me who You are that I can walk hand in hand with You. *14 And he said, My presence shall go with thee, and I will give thee rest.* God promised to turn His face towards Moses, and to give him His attention. *15 And he said unto him, If thy presence go not with me, carry us not up hence. 16 For wherein shall it be known here that I and thy people have found grace in thy sight? Is it not in that thou goest with us? So shall we be separated, I and thy people, from all the people that are upon the face of the earth.* Moses said it is your presence that marks us as your own and distinguishes us from the rest of the world. Give us an ever increasing revelation of your presence and your glory. *17 And the LORD said unto Moses, I will do this thing also that thou hast spoken: for thou hast found grace in my sight, and I know thee by name. 18 And he said, I beseech thee, shew me thy glory.* Glory here is Strong's Hebrew word

3513 ***kabod*** which includes His weighty splendor, honor and revealed glory. Moses said show me who you are, don't hide anything from me. I want to know you Lord. *19 And he said, I will make all my goodness pass before thee, and I will proclaim the name of the LORD before thee; and will be gracious to whom I will be gracious, and will shew mercy on whom I will shew mercy.* God was willing that His character and a portion of His glory be revealed to this one who sought Him out and hungered for more revelation. That principle still stands today. If we want His presence and His glory we have to seek Him out. We have to walk in what is already revealed to us and ask for more. God will not chastise us for wanting more of Him. He delights in it. *20 And he said, Thou canst not see my face: for there shall no man see me, and live. 21 And the LORD said, Behold, there is a place by me, and thou shalt stand upon a rock: 22 And it shall come to pass, while my glory passeth by, that I will put thee in a clift of the rock, and will cover thee with my hand while I pass by: 23 And I will take away mine hand, and thou shalt see my back parts: but my face shall not be seen.* God revealed Himself to Moses.

**Exodus 34:1-8 (KJV)** *1 And the LORD said unto Moses, Hew thee two tables of stone like unto the first: and I will write upon these tables the words that were in the first tables, which thou brakest. 2 And be ready in the morning, and come up in the morning unto mount Sinai, and present thyself there to me in the top of the mount. 3 And no man shall come up with thee, neither let any man be seen throughout all the mount; neither let the flocks nor herds feed before that mount. 4 And he hewed two tables of stone like unto the first; and Moses rose up early in the morning, and went up unto mount Sinai, as the LORD had commanded Him, and took in His hand the two tables of stone. 5 And the LORD descended in the cloud, and stood with Him there, and proclaimed the* *name of the LORD. 6 And the LORD passed by before Him, and proclaimed, The LORD, The LORD God, merciful and gracious, longsuffering, and abundant in goodness and truth, 7 Keeping mercy for thousands, forgiving iniquity and transgression and sin, and that will by no means clear the guilty; visiting the iniquity of the fathers upon the children, and upon the children's children, unto the third and to the fourth generation. 8 And Moses made haste, and bowed his head toward the earth, and worshipped.* Moses physically climbed the mountain, and he physically carved the stone tablets. But he could not see with his natural eyes the fullness of the One he loved. He bowed his heart and mind and body down to worship the revelation of the Lord in limited glory. We too climb in the spirit, and bow down our hearts and worship the Lord our God. It is an awesome thing to come before Him. He is calling you to draw near. Will you respond and make the effort to climb the mountain into His presence?

## Presence Demands Obedience

If we are seeking the presence of God, we cannot be walking in rebellion, or disobedience, or sin. Those seem like strong words, but that is exactly the place we are in when we do not follow closely to God's written instructions. Jesus said we prove our love by walking it out daily. If you love the Lord you will obey. Obey has a negative connotation to some people; they do not want to hear it, but it is an essential step towards unity with God. You will never make it up the mountain without controlling your thoughts, words and actions.

Jesus was our example, and our teacher. Look what He said concerning obedience. **John 8:28-32 (KJV)** *28 Then said Jesus unto them, When ye have lifted up the Son of man, then shall ye know that I am he, and that I do nothing of myself; but as my Father hath taught me, I speak these things.* Jesus first saw and heard what the Father wanted and then did it. He openly gave credit to the Father, saying I do just what He says. *29 And he that sent me is with me: the Father hath not left me alone; for I do always those things that please Him.* Jesus linked obedience and presence. He said His response to instructions from His Father was to obey and that because He obeyed, the Father was perpetually with Him. It makes sense to imply that disobedience would have hindered that unity. *30 As he spake these words, many believed on him. 31 Then said Jesus to those Jews which believed on him, If ye continue in my word, then are ye my disciples indeed; 32 And ye shall know the truth, and the truth shall make you free.* He did not stutter when He said it. If you love Jesus you will obey Him on a continual basis.

**John 14:21 (KJV)** *21 He that hath my commandments, and keepeth them, he it is that loveth me: and he that loveth me shall be loved of my Father, and I will love him, and will manifest myself to him.* Jesus clearly stated that obedience is the basis for relationship. God does not force us to obey. He allows us to make a choice; He has given us a free will. Generally speaking, people resist the idea of obedience. They do not want to be told what to do. Even a toddler will demand independence. "I will do it myself—I will do it my way." Just like those children many people stubbornly refuse instructions and walk in selfish rebellion. The reason most people do not want to obey is that they fear someone will be dictatorial with them. They fear an abuse of power. God does not manipulate or take advantage of anyone. God is not going to force you to do anything that is not good for you. We can have confidence in the heart of God which will help us to surrender our will to His. If we want to walk with God, we have to learn to fully and willingly submit to His will.

The Matthew Henry Commentary states that obedience is the carrying out of the word and will of another person, especially the will of God. Obedience is the active response to what we know God has spoken. Both New Testament and Old Testament teachings relate the idea that we receive revelation and instruction from God, and then do as God instructed. That obedience makes us eligible for the next revelation. **James 1:22 (KJV)** *22 But be ye doers of the word, and not hearers only, deceiving your own selves.* Knowledge demands obedience. We become accountable when we know to do good or to avoid evil. **James 4:17 (KJV)** *17 Therefore to him that knoweth to do good, and doeth it not, to him it is sin.* When we fail to obey we place ourselves in a position to be judged. Lord, please help us to both hear and obey. **Psalm 143:10 (KJV)** *10 Teach me to do thy will; for thou art my God: thy spirit is good; lead me into the land of uprightness.*

David cherished the Word of the Lord and found it was good to walk in obedience. **Psalm 119:97-106 (KJV)** *97 O how love I thy law! It is my meditation all the day. 98 Thou through thy commandments hast made me wiser than mine enemies: for they are ever with me. 99 I have more understanding than all my teachers: for thy testimonies are my meditation. 100 I understand more than the ancients, because I keep thy precepts. 101 I have refrained my feet from every evil way, that I might keep thy word. 102 I have not departed from thy judgments: for thou hast taught me. 103 How sweet are thy words unto my taste! Yea, sweeter than honey to my mouth! 104 Through thy precepts I get understanding: therefore I hate every false way. 105 Thy word is a lamp unto my feet, and a light unto my path. 106 I have sworn, and I will perform it, that I will keep thy righteous judgments.*

Obedience is a strong underlying theme of the Word of God. It is an important topic for all believers. God warned us that if we rebel we will be judged, but if we obey we can walk in the blessing. **Romans 12:1-2 (NIV)** *1 Therefore, I urge you, brothers and sisters, in view of God's mercy, to* *offer your bodies as a living sacrifice, holy and pleasing to God—this is your true and proper worship. 2 Do not conform to the pattern of this world, but be transformed by the renewing of your mind. Then you will be able to test and approve what God's will is—his good, pleasing and perfect will.* Obedience will make us able to both know and do what pleases the Lord and it is our job as Christians to represent Him well. We want others to see us walk in a way that honors Him. He said you tell your body what it can and cannot do, you tell your mind what it is allowed to meditate on—you choose to walk out your faith. Your obedience is an offering of worship.

**Matthew 21:28-31 (KJV)** *28 But what think ye? A certain man had two sons; and he came to the first, and said, Son, go work to day in my vineyard. 29 He answered and said, I will not: but afterward he repented, and went. 30 And he came to the second, and said likewise. And he answered and said, I go, sir: and went not. 31 Whether of them twain did the will of his father?* It was not the one who said, I will, but the one who actually went that pleased and obeyed his father. We usually plan to do well, but sometimes we fail to follow through. Even the Apostle Paul struggled against His own flesh. [Romans 7:14-24] Our plan to obey is not enough we have to find a way to really do what the Lord has told us to do.

**Isaiah 1:19 (KJV)** 1*9 If ye be willing and obedient, ye shall eat the good of the land:* "Notice He doesn't say just obedient, but rather willing and obedient. Willingness deals with the attitude of our heart." (Bevere, p. 117) The heart is always more important to God than our mere actions. "We seek to carry out His wishes as if they were our own. We take His heart's desires on as our own. This is true obedience." (Bevere, p. 111) Think about it like this illustration. There was a little boy that was overly active in the classroom. The teacher got permission from his mother to literally hold him in his seat. After a few days he was compliant in body, but he told his friend, "I might be sitting on the outside, but I am standing on the inside." Sometimes we are like that, forced to function as directed, but still rebelling within. That is not obedience, because the willing aspect is missing.

In Deuteronomy Moses brought the people the law. They were fearful to hear it for themselves, so they sent Moses. **Deuteronomy 5:27-29 (KJV)** *27 Go thou near, and hear all that the LORD our God shall say: and speak thou unto us all that the LORD our God shall speak unto thee; and we will hear it, and do it. 28 And the LORD heard the voice of your words, when ye spake unto me; and the LORD said unto me, I have heard the voice of the words of this people, which they have spoken unto thee: they have well said all that they have spoken. 29 <u>O that there were such an heart in them, that they would fear me, and keep all my commandments always, that it might be well with them,</u> and with their children for ever!* Those people promised a heart that would lead them to obey. God suggested that if they would keep the first commandment which was to love Him with all their heart and soul and strength, they would have done better with the other nine. We have a similar New Testament reference. **Matthew 22:36-40 (KJV)** *36 Master, which is the great commandment in the law? 37 Jesus said unto Him, Thou shalt love the Lord thy God with all thy heart, and with all thy soul, and with all thy mind. 38 This is the first and great commandment. 39 And the second is like unto it, Thou shalt love thy neighbour as thyself. 40 On these two commandments hang all the law and the prophets.* God cares about the heart of man. Do not work harder to follow the law, just love deeper. When the heart of man is committed to the Lord, he will desire the things that please

God and obedience will flow naturally. Climb higher, get closer to the God who loves you. Moses admonished the people to follow closely. **Deuteronomy 30:20 (NIV)** *20 and that you may love the LORD your God, listen to his voice, and hold fast to him. For the LORD is your life...* All that is good in this life comes from God and if we will harken to His voice and obey Him—He will be with us.

**John 14:23-24 (KJV)** *23 Jesus answered and said unto him, If a man love me, he will keep my words: and my Father will love him, and we will come unto him, and make our abode with him. 24 He that loveth me not keepeth not my sayings: and the word which ye hear is not mine, but the Father's which sent me.* Jesus made sure that we knew that His word must be our final authority; it must be obeyed. We say we are His, we claim we love Him, but our actions speak louder than our words. **John 14:15 (KJV)** *15 If ye love me, keep my commandments.* He said nothing that indicates we can add our own slant to that, or modify it to fit our situation. God is unchanging. The Word of God stands steadfast and sure. What is right and good will not change, and what is sin will not either.

In the Old Testament God called Saul to be king and He said to him go and kill everything alive in the city. Saul went and walked in partial obedience, that partial obedience was seen as sin and it cost him the kingdom. **1 Samuel 15:4-9 (KJV)** *4 And Saul gathered the people together, and numbered them in Telaim, two hundred thousand footmen, and ten thousand men of Judah. 5 And Saul came to a city of Amalek, and laid wait in the valley... 7 And Saul smote the Amalekites from Havilah until thou comest to Shur, that is over against Egypt. 8 And he took Agag the king of the Amalekites alive, and utterly destroyed all the people with the edge of the sword. 9 But Saul and the people spared*

*Agag, and the best of the sheep, and of the oxen, and of the fatlings, and the lambs, and all that was good, and would not utterly destroy them: but every thing that was vile and refuse, that they destroyed utterly.* He did most of what God required, but not all. Any other time the things he did would have been standard operating procedure. He did what most conquering leaders did. The victor was usually entitled to the spoils of war. Anything of value would have been taken to camp and divided among the winning army. The fallen king would have been marched through the city as a sign of dominance. It humiliated the fallen nation and built up the triumphant army—it gave them street credibility. This time, however, the Lord specifically told them to kill every person, kill every animal and to destroy everything. Saul did not obey.

Look what his self-will cost him. **1 Samuel 15:10-23 (KJV)** *10 Then came the word of the LORD unto Samuel, saying, 11 It repenteth me that I have set up Saul to be king: for he is turned back from following me, and hath not performed my commandments. And it grieved Samuel; and he cried unto the LORD all night. 12 And when Samuel rose early to meet Saul in the morning, it was told Samuel, saying, Saul came to Carmel, and, behold, he set him up a place, and is gone about, and passed on, and gone down to Gilgal. 13 And Samuel came to Saul: and Saul said unto him, Blessed be thou of the LORD: I have performed the commandment of the LORD.* He lied to the prophet of God. In those days a prophet was called a seer, didn't Saul know that Samuel would discern his lie. *14 And Samuel said, What meaneth then this bleating of the sheep in mine ears, and the lowing of the oxen which I hear? 15 And Saul said, They have brought them from the Amalekites: for the people spared the best of the sheep and of the oxen, to sacrifice unto the LORD* *thy God; and the rest we have utterly destroyed. 16 Then Samuel said unto Saul, Stay, and I will tell thee what the LORD hath said to me this night. And he said unto him, Say on. 17 And Samuel said, When thou wast little in thine own sight, wast thou not made the head of the tribes of Israel, and the LORD anointed thee king over Israel? 18 And the LORD sent thee on a journey, and said, Go and utterly destroy the sinners the Amalekites, and fight against them until they be consumed. 19 Wherefore then didst thou not obey the voice of the LORD, but didst fly upon the spoil, and didst evil in the sight of the LORD? 20 And Saul said unto Samuel, Yea, I have obeyed the voice of the LORD, and have gone the way which the LORD sent me, and have brought Agag the king of Amalek, and have utterly destroyed the Amalekites. 21 But the people took of the spoil, sheep and oxen, the chief of the things which should have been utterly destroyed, to sacrifice unto the LORD thy God in Gilgal.* Saul did not repent; he lied claiming he had obeyed. Then Saul blamed the soldiers. He even tried to make it sound religious. His heart was so hardened toward God that he could excuse his behavior without guilt. *22 And Samuel said, Hath the LORD as great delight in burnt offerings and sacrifices, as in obeying the voice of the LORD? Behold, to obey is better than sacrifice, and to hearken than the fat of rams. 23 For rebellion is as the sin of witchcraft, and stubbornness is as iniquity and idolatry. Because thou hast rejected the word of the LORD, he hath also rejected thee from being king.* God did not see it as a slight variation in plan; God called it rebellion and sin. God never expects us to be perfect, but He does expect us to passionately seek Him and to choose to obey Him when we have specific instructions.

The fullest blessings of God are dependent upon obedience. You can pray and fast and study and still miss the fullness of His blessings if you are refusing to do anything He has told you. If you feel distanced from God go back to the place where you were last in obedience, and start walking from there, the path will become clear. Wherever you got off the path, find out which way He wanted you to go, and then just climb. His ways are sure. He has walked this path before and you can know that He will guide you perfectly.

Obedience is a life principle; it is a faithful, continuous listening to His voice. We walk with Him daily. It is not a one time and I am finished event. Salvation was a beginning not an end of commitment. God wants us to live a life of habitual obedience. Even Jesus had to walk in obedience. **Hebrews 5:8-9 (KJV)** *8 Though he were a Son, yet learned he obedience by the things which he suffered; 9 And being made perfect, he became the author of eternal salvation unto <u>all them that obey Him</u>;* **Hebrews 10:8-9 (KJV)** *8... Sacrifice and offering and burnt offerings and offering for sin thou wouldest not, neither hadst pleasure therein; which are offered by the law; 9 Then said he, Lo, I come to do thy will, O God. He taketh away the first, that he may establish the second.* Jesus came in order to fulfill the will of the Father. His entire purpose was to become the sacrifice that would bring us to the Father. If Jesus, the Son of God came to obey and suffered during that obedience in order to make us His, we must also obey whether it is comfortable and convenient or not.

**1 Samuel 3:1 (KJV)** *1 And the child Samuel ministered unto the LORD before Eli. And the word of the LORD was precious in those days; there was no open vision.* The New International Version says the word of the Lord was rare. That means they were not receiving fresh revelation. Why would God withhold revelation? All revelation including understanding the things of the Spirit and the written Scriptures are dependent upon God's presence. When we welcome Him, He speaks to us. Where there is little presence there is little revelation. When there is little obedience, there is also little presence. That is why there was a rare word from the Lord. Insight and manifest are directly linked to time in His presence. **John 14:23 (KJV)** *23 Jesus answered and said unto him, If a man love me, he will keep my words: and my Father will love him, and we will come unto him, and make our abode with him.* That is what we want, His fullness living in and with us. We will learn more from Him by spending time with Him.

**Philippians 2:4-8 (KJV)** *4 Look not every man on His own things, but every man also on the things of others. 5 Let this mind be in you, which was also in Christ Jesus: 6 Who, being in the form of God, thought it not robbery to be equal with God: 7 But made himself of no reputation, and took upon him the form of a servant, and was made in the likeness of men: 8 And being found in fashion as a man, he humbled himself, and became obedient unto death, even the death of the cross.* Jesus was the prime example of humility and obedience. We were instructed to follow His example and adopt His attitude.

According to John the identifying characteristic of a believer is that we walk in obedience. **1 John 2:3-6 (KJV)** *3 And hereby we do know that we know him, if we keep his commandments. 4 He that saith, I know him, and keepeth not his commandments, is a liar, and the truth is not in him. 5 But whoso keepeth his word, in him verily is the love of God perfected: hereby know we that we are in him. 6 He that saith he abideth in him ought himself also so to walk, even as he walked.* John, the closest disciple of Christ, tells us that as believers we are now the brothers and sisters of Jesus. We were purchased by the blood, and adopted into the family of

God. It is our obligation to live like Jesus and to act in a way that will draw others to Christ, not turn them away.

**Hebrews 11:1 (KJV)** *1 Now faith is the substance of things hoped for, the evidence of things not seen.* The whole chapter in Hebrews 11 tells us of men and women who followed God. They obeyed when it seemed impossible. The only evidence they had was their trust in the relationship they had with God. **Hebrews 11: 6 (KJV)** *6 But without faith it is impossible to please him: for he that cometh to God must believe that he is, and that he is a rewarder of them that diligently seek him.* Noah preached for 120 years while he built the ark with not a single convert. Abraham traveled to an unknown location because God said go. Years later he also offered his son as a sacrifice. There is a huge list of men of faith and then the Scripture says that none of them got all that was promised to them in their lifetime. **Hebrews 11:13 (KJV)** *13 These all died in faith, not having received the promises, but having seen them afar off, and were persuaded of them, and embraced them, and confessed that they were strangers and pilgrims on the earth.* They all died still believing, that is the testimony we want to leave. We walk it out every day of our lives and if part of the manifestation takes place after we have gone it is alright.

We call ourselves Christians, but that name means nothing if we are not listening to Christ and living by His instructions. We are the ones called by name, who live in His presence and that alone distinguishes us from all other people. It is not enough that we go to church. There is no value in proclaiming ourselves as His, until we walk in fellowship with Him.

I have known believers who rebel when they feel like men or even God is demanding obedience. "The more you focus on the things you must not do, the more power they have over you. Holiness is not a set of do's and don'ts." (Prince, p. 23) Walking with God requires that we seek to please Him. It is not hard to obey someone who you know loves you. We are not following rules, but our Father. Our hearts determine our actions and we focus on the one we love and our hearts control our actions. **Jeremiah 7:23 (KJV)** *23 But this thing commanded I them, saying, Obey my voice, and I will be your God, and ye shall be my people: and walk ye in all the ways that I have commanded you, that it may be well unto you.* God is wise and all powerful and holy. Obeying Him makes our lives better, so we choose to obey and honor Him.

## Give Me that Mountain

**Romans 1:17 (KJV)** *17 For therein is the righteousness of God revealed from faith to faith: as it is written, The just shall live by faith.* What do we really mean when we say faith? If we are in faith, we are fully persuaded of the integrity of God and His Word. Strong's defines faith, in the Scripture we just quoted as, assurance, belief, constancy, and moral conviction in the truthfulness of God. It is the committing of the whole person upon the integrity of the Almighty. [Strong's Greek word #3982 *pistis*] That is the kind of faith we are examining here. Faith is the confident knowledge that God, who can never change and never lie, will keep His Covenant promises to us because we fully rely upon Him. That is the faith that urged Caleb to say "Give me that mountain."

The children of Israel had arrived at the border of the Promised Land. Moses sent out twelve men, one from each tribe. They were to scout the land and determine the value of it and the strength of its cities and fortifications. They had already been told the land was theirs. Two men stood and gave an honest assessment. Both Joshua and Caleb wanted to go in and take their possession immediately. The other ten spies were shouting about the enormity of the opposition. They feared they could not take the land or fight against the giants because they looked only in the natural. God called their fear and the words they spoke an 'evil report.' It was evil because it contradicted what God had promised. They did not put their confidence in the One who promised. They confessed exactly what they believed, that God was not great enough to give them the victory. Those ten men died for their lack of faith.

Caleb knew that with God all things were possible. He had the kind of faith that pleased God. That kind of faith is a full reliance upon and confidence in the Lord. When offered the chance to stand up for God, Caleb did. He spoke it, because he believed it. The Hebrew people put great stock in the meaning of names. It is funny to me that Caleb meant dog or slave, but he did not live down to his name. He chose to serve God with such integrity that he became a trusted leader. Caleb was a powerful man of faith, and his words and actions proved it. He and Joshua were the only two who stood up as men of faith to take hold of the promise of God and were willing to go into battle knowing that God would be with them.

**Numbers 13:30-33 (KJV)** *30 And Caleb stilled the people before Moses, and said, Let us go up at once, and possess it; for we are well able to overcome it.* He could say that because in his heart he recognized the covenant factor. God was with them. God had said, "Take the land for I have given it to you." How could they lose if God already ordained victory? Caleb trusted in the faithfulness of an almighty God. Caleb never said there are no giants; he said we are able if God is with us. There are always going to be obstacles but they must not change what we believe. *31 But the men that went up with him said, We be not able to go up against the people; for they are stronger than we. 32 And they brought up an evil report of the land which they had searched unto the children of Israel, saying, The land, through which we have gone to search it, is a land that eateth up the inhabitants thereof; and all the people that we saw in it are men of a great stature. 33 And there we saw the giants, the sons of Anak, which come of the giants: and we were in our own sight as grasshoppers, and so we were in their sight.* How you see yourself determines your destiny. Caleb believed he was in covenant with a God who would make him successful. Those other men saw every inch of that mountain as treacherous, and their real enemy was fear. They could not win because they believed they were no more powerful than insects about to be squashed.

**Numbers 14:5-9 (KJV)** *5 Then Moses and Aaron fell on their faces before all the assembly of the congregation of the children of Israel. 6 And Joshua the son of Nun, and Caleb the son of Jephunneh, which were of them that searched the land, rent their clothes:* Joshua and Caleb both showed an outward sign of mourning. The people needed to see the depth of their concern over the rebellion. *7 And they spake unto all the company of the children of Israel, saying, The land, which we passed through to search it, is an exceeding good land. 8 If the LORD delight in us, then he will bring us into this land, and give it us; a land which floweth with milk and honey.* They believed with God's help they could more than gain victory over the local army, they could fully possess the land. *9 Only rebel not ye against the LORD, neither fear ye the people of the land; for they are bread for us: their defence is departed from them, and the*

*LORD is with us: fear them not.* Caleb said we will eat this people up. He was trying to get their focus back on God and His promises. The enemy armies are never a match for us with God on our side.

**Numbers 14:20-24 (KJV)** *20 And the LORD said, I have pardoned according to thy word; 21 But as truly as I live, all the earth shall be filled with the glory of the LORD. 22 Because all those men which have seen my glory, and my miracles, which I did in Egypt and in the wilderness, and have tempted me now these ten times, and have not hearkened to my voice; 23 Surely they shall not see the land which I sware unto their fathers, neither shall any of them that provoked me see it: 24 But my servant Caleb, because he had another spirit with him, and hath <u>followed me fully</u>, him will I bring into the land whereinto he went; and his seed shall possess it.* That is exactly what happened, one by one those rebellious unbelieving men all died off. By the time the land was being divided up it just Joshua and Caleb who had ever seen it firsthand. "Caleb was a success in God because he totally dedicated himself to following God… That means Caleb did everything God told him to do. He believed what God said, he said what God said, and he did what God said. He was in agreement with God in every area of his life." (Hagin Jr. p.83)

**Joshua 14:6-14 (KJV)** *6 Then the children of Judah came unto Joshua in Gilgal: and Caleb the son of Jephunneh the Kenezite said unto Him, Thou knowest the thing that the LORD said unto Moses the man of God concerning me and thee in Kadeshbarnea. 7 Forty years old was I when Moses the servant of the LORD sent me from Kadeshbarnea to espy out the land; and I brought him word again as it was in mine heart. 8 Nevertheless my brethren that went up with me made the heart of the people melt: but I wholly followed the LORD my God. 9 And Moses sware* *on that day, saying, Surely the land whereon thy feet have trodden shall be thine inheritance, and thy children's for ever, because thou hast wholly followed the LORD my God. 10 And now, behold, the LORD hath kept me alive, as he said, these forty and five years, even since the LORD spake this word unto Moses, while the children of Israel wandered in the wilderness: and now, lo, I am this day fourscore and five years old. 11 As yet I am as strong this day as I was in the day that Moses sent me: as my strength was then, even so is my strength now, for war, both to go out, and to come in. <u>12 Now therefore give me this mountain, whereof the LORD spake in that day</u>; for thou heardest in that day how the Anakims were there, and that the cities were great and fenced: if so be the LORD will be with me, then I shall be able to drive them out, as the LORD said. 13 And Joshua blessed him, and gave unto Caleb the son of Jephunneh Hebron for an inheritance. 14 Hebron therefore became the inheritance of Caleb the son of Jephunneh the Kenezite unto this day, because that he wholly followed the LORD God of Israel.* That was mountain possessing faith. Caleb was 85 years old. He had watched a whole generation die, but he still believed the promise of God. Confidence in the living God made him able to do above and beyond what was possible in the natural. "Caleb set about to accomplish what God had said even though he was deterred and detained for many years. It's too bad some believers today don't have that kind of tenacious faith!" (Hagin Jr p. 88)

    Have you ever asked God for a mountain? Maybe you did not ask for a literal mountain, but for something that was too big to be possible without Him. I have believed to receive a job, and a miraculous healing more than once. I have had to stand my ground for the life of my child. I have asked for protection during a tornado and the restoration of my marriage when my husband wanted a divorce, those were all mountains at the time. None of those things were easy, but I believed that I knew the will of God and I purposed to trust Him. That kind of faith pleases God. **Hebrews 11:6 (KJV)** *6 But without faith it is impossible to please him: for he that cometh to God must believe that he is, and that he is a rewarder of them that diligently seek him.* Joshua and Caleb trusted like Abraham did. They put all their hope and confidence in God and God proved He was trustworthy. **Romans 4:20-22 (KJV)** *20 He staggered not at the promise of God through unbelief; but was strong in faith, giving glory to God; 21 And being fully persuaded that, what he had promised, he was able also to perform. 22 And therefore it was imputed to him for righteousness.* That is faith that works and faith that God will honor.

God is not bothered by your requests. He knows you have needs and like any good parent He wants to meet your needs. Actually He wants you blessed above and beyond what you could ask for. He allowed us entrance into His presence so we could draw strength and faith from Him. He wants you to come to Him, and He wants to meet your needs. He wanted Caleb to have his mountain, and He wants you to conquer yours as well.

**1 John 5:14-15 (KJV)** *14 And this is the confidence that we have in him, that, if we ask any thing according to his will, he heareth us: 15 And if we know that he hear us, whatsoever we ask, we know that we have the petitions that we desired of him.* **John 14:14 (KJV)** *14 If ye shall ask any thing in my name, I will do it.* That sounds like He was saying, 'Nothing is too big and nothing is too small to bring to Him.' We are to cast the whole of our care on Him and ask in faith believing. "That word ask here in the Greek means to demand. You are not demanding it of Jesus, but you are demanding it as Peter demanded the man at the beautiful gate to rise and walk." (Kenyon, p. 117) You base your authority on Jesus and you can have what you say.

**Mark 11:19-24 (KJV)** *19 And when even was come, he went out of the city. 20 And in the morning, as they passed by, they saw the fig tree dried up from the roots. 21 And Peter calling to remembrance saith unto Him, Master, behold, the* *fig tree which thou cursedst is withered away. 22 And Jesus answering saith unto them, Have faith in God. 23 For verily I say unto you, That whosoever shall say unto this mountain, Be thou removed, and be thou cast into the sea; and shall not doubt in his heart, but shall believe that those things which he saith shall come to pass; he shall have whatsoever he saith. 24 Therefore I say unto you, What things soever ye desire, when ye pray, believe that ye receive them, and ye shall have them.*

**John 15:7-8 (KJV)** *7 If ye abide in me, and my words abide in you, ye shall ask what ye will, and it shall be done unto you. 8 Herein is my Father glorified, that ye bear much fruit; so shall ye be my disciples.* It honors and pleases God when we ask for what will increase His kingdom and bless His people.

We come to the Lord, knowing His promises and reaching out to accept what He has said is ours. We come boldly because we are confident that He is and that He loves us. **Mark 9:23 (KJV)** *23 Jesus said unto Him, If thou canst believe, all things are possible to Him that believeth.* That Scripture, taken in context gives us another key to faith. God never responds to need alone. God is moved by, and responds to faith. A father brings His son for healing, and asks Jesus to help, but then adds a "but" and an "if" to His request. **Mark 9:22- 24 (KJV)** *...but if thou canst do any thing, have compassion on us, and help us. 23 Jesus said unto Him, If thou canst believe, all things are possible to Him that believeth. 24 And straightway the father of the child cried out, and said with tears, Lord, I believe; help thou mine unbelief.* This father was honest enough to say, I am using all the faith I have just to come. Help me where I falter, strengthen the faith I have and drive out whatever doubts I have. That man left with a son healed. Just like him, we find Jesus to be willing, able, faithful and trustworthy.

**Matthew 21:22 (KJV)** *22 And all things, whatsoever ye shall ask in prayer, believing, ye shall receive.* You do the believing before the asking. We are told to have faith, to believe. Believe is a verb. It has requires action. Faith works for us, when we respond to the truth. In the case of salvation, believing Jesus is the savior is just a theory until He becomes your savior. The Scriptures clearly tell us that Jesus died for our sins. **Romans 10:9 (KJV)** *9 That if thou shalt confess with thy mouth the Lord Jesus, and shalt believe in thine heart that God hath raised him from the dead, thou shalt be saved.* When we acted upon that it became powerful enough to change our destiny and the very essence of our being. All faith works the same way. First you find out God has promised it. You believe it is so. You say it, and start acting like it is already yours and then the manifestation comes. The world has it all wrong, they say, "Seeing is believing." The truth is that, believing is seeing.

**Hebrews 11:1 (KJV)** *1 Now faith is the substance of things hoped for, the evidence of things not seen.* Faith must always be in the present tense. God has already sent Jesus. Jesus already shed His blood. He already promised to give us what we need. It is not going to happen someday it is mine now. Hope looks to the future but faith takes possession right now.

**Psalm 37:3-5 (KJV)** *3 Trust in the LORD, and do good; so shalt thou dwell in the land, and verily thou shalt be fed. 4 Delight thyself also in the LORD; and he shall give thee the desires of thine heart. 5 Commit thy way unto the LORD; trust also in him; and he shall bring it to pass.* The author of this psalm used the words trust and commit to clarify his stance of faith. Those are key aspects in walking out what we believe. Confidence in God and a determination to walk with Him will continually bring results.

**Matthew 14:23-33 (KJV)** *23 And when he had sent the multitudes away, he went up into a mountain apart to pray: and when the evening was come, he was there alone.* There is the Lord going to the mountain again to pray. *24 But the ship was now in the midst of the sea, tossed with waves: for the wind was contrary. 25 And in the fourth watch of the night Jesus went unto them, walking on the sea. 26 And when the disciples saw him walking on the sea, they were troubled, saying, It is a spirit; and they cried out for fear. 27 But straightway Jesus spake unto them, saying, Be of good cheer; it is I; be not afraid. 28 And Peter answered him and said, Lord, if it be thou, bid me come unto thee on the water.* Real faith does not require past experience to rely on God. Peter knew it was impossible to walk on water. Notice the text does not say let me walk on the water. It does not indicate he wanted some amazing experience. He asked Jesus to invite him to come closer, "Call me to you." *29 And he said, Come. And when Peter was come down out of the ship, he walked on the water, to go to Jesus.* He knew there was a storm, and he knew water could not hold him up. Peter understood that to do so was to violate all the laws of nature, but he got out of the boat anyway. Peter wanted to be where Jesus was. It is not presumption if you wait for the call and then obey. That is faith. The eleven reasonable men were still in the boat, fearful of the storm and probably thinking Peter was as good as dead. Peter is acting as if that water is solid ground. Acting as if what God said is true and just doing what you would if that were the case is a real definition of faith. Peter was walking on the water, drawing nearer to the Lord, when he let his senses take over. *30 But when he saw the wind boisterous, he was afraid; and beginning to sink, he cried, saying, Lord, save me. 31 And immediately Jesus stretched forth his hand, and caught him, and said unto him, O thou of little faith, wherefore didst thou doubt?* Peter had already walked some distance. He had already exercised his faith when he became overwhelmed by the circumstances. He took his eyes off the Master for just a second, and he started to sink. If we want to stand in faith, or walk in faith, we must keep our eyes steadfastly on the One who is the truth. Jesus said Peter had little faith; He did not say Peter was faithless. Peter had enough faith to begin walking. He cried out in fear, but then he took the hand of Jesus and walked the rest of the way. *32 And when they were come into the ship, the wind ceased. 33 Then they that were in the ship came and worshipped Him, saying, Of a truth thou art the Son of God.* Sense knowledge will always try to assert itself against the faith walk. If you have to choose between what you see and feel and think and your past experience or your opportunity to follow the Lord—choose to go with faith in God.

Real faith causes the inward man to grow until the outward man responds. We should never be moved by what we sense, but only by what we truly believe. We can trust God and His word over all of our education and experience. I have often been wrong, but God is always right.

You can only believe what you think is possible. **Romans 10:17 (KJV)** *17 So then faith cometh by hearing, and hearing by the word of God.* If you read it in the Bible, it is true. Faith takes hold of the promises of God. Actually, faith comes by hearing and hearing the word continually. It comes by reading it and saying it until it becomes a part of you. Faith rests in the confident assurance of His faithfulness. **Hebrews 10:23 (KJV)** *23 Let us hold fast the profession of our faith without wavering; (for he is faithful that promised;)* Keep climbing, with the full assurance that God will keep you safe.

If you want to see your needs met, there are hundreds of promises in the word of God, take one and make it yours. Determine that the Bible is true and hold to it like a man clinging to the side of a mountain. Do not loosen your grip. Do not look down. Put your full trust in God alone. Look into the face of God and you will have the confidence to say "Give me my mountain." Like Caleb you can take possession of all God has promised you. "Mountain-taking is not for those who are afraid to skin their knees from trying to climb up the mountainside of their possession…It is not for those who take the easy way out. But when you finally reach the top of that mountain, what a thrill of victory you'll experience. (Hagin Jr. p. 103)

Hebrews 11:1 1 *Now faith is the substance of things hoped for, the evidence of things not seen.*

Mark 11:24 (KJV) *24 Therefore I say unto you, What things soever ye desire, when ye pray, believe that ye receive them, and ye shall have them*

## Faith That Works

There is something to be said about standing your ground in faith. I think of it as stubborn faith—it won't back down, and won't give up. That kind of faith is grounded in time with God over His written word or in sustained times of prayer. Even Jesus sometimes spent the whole night praying. We will never accomplish much with a five minute prayer. We need to understand what it says in Hebrews. **Hebrews 11:1 (KJV)** *1 Now faith is the substance of things hoped for, the evidence of things not seen.* We are not really walking in faith until we have held fast to God and His promise, with no other assurance. We have no proof but we trust God for what we need. That confidence becomes concrete hard and produces what we asked for. Faith is always now—it is always present tense. It is not about what will be, but about our spiritual grasp on what we believe God already promised us. Faith demands that we cling to the truth and refuse to turn away from Him.

Jacob wrestled with the angel all night and because he would not give in when it was hard, he received a blessing. **Genesis 32:24-28 (KJV)** *24 And Jacob was left alone; and there wrestled a man with him until the breaking of the day. 25 And when he saw that he prevailed not against him, he* *touched the hollow of his thigh; and the hollow of Jacob's thigh was out of joint, as he wrestled with him. 26 And he said, Let me go, for the day breaketh. And he said, I will not let thee go, except thou bless me.* Jacob was injured in the struggle but his determination held firm. *27 And he said unto him, What is thy name? And he said, Jacob. 28 And he said, Thy name shall be called no more Jacob, but Israel: for as a prince hast thou power with God and with men, and hast prevailed.* The prayer of perseverance changed His name and His character. Jacob meant deceiver. Israel meant God strives, or in more modern day language, God's victorious one.

As believers we must learn to hold fast, while we wait for what we have asked to manifest. **Mark 11:24 (KJV)** *24 Therefore I say unto you, What things soever ye desire, when ye pray, believe that ye receive them, and ye shall have them.* The Bible teaches us to believe, then to ask and then to keep hold of the promise until it is ours. Faith really is mostly just not giving in until we get what we were promised. That is actually part of a longer passage so we will look at it again and expand upon what we have already established.

**Mark 11:12-24 (KJV)** *12 And on the morrow, when they were come from Bethany, he was hungry: 13 And seeing a fig tree afar off having leaves, he came, if haply he might find any thing thereon: and when he came to it, he found nothing but leaves; for the time of figs was not yet.* It is reasonable to expect figs even early in the season if there are leaves, because the leaves came in after the fruit. The tree appeared to be productive, but it was useless. *14 And Jesus answered and said unto it, No man eat fruit of thee hereafter for ever. And his disciples heard it... 20 And in the morning, as they passed by, they saw the fig tree dried up from the roots. 21 And Peter calling to remembrance saith* *unto him, Master, behold, the fig tree which thou cursedst is withered away. 22 And Jesus answering saith unto them, Have faith in God.* He was teaching them what the God kind of faith was. *23 For verily I say unto you, That whosoever shall say unto this mountain, Be thou removed, and be thou cast into the sea; and shall not doubt in his heart, but shall believe that those things which he <u>saith</u> shall come to pass; he shall have whatsoever he <u>saith</u>. 24 <u>Therefore I say unto you, What things soever ye desire, when ye pray, believe that ye receive them, and ye shall have them</u>.* Kenneth Hagin said it was the God kind of faith, when the person both believes in the heart and says with his mouth what he believes will happen. "That is the same kind of faith God used to create the worlds in the beginning. He simply believed that what He said would come to pass…and it did." (Hagin p. 4)

"To successfully receive everything that God has for you in this life, you've got to say what God says: I am more than a conqueror through Christ who loves me. I am a victor, because greater is He that is in me, than he that is in the world. Nothing is impossible with God! Either you have a big God and a little devil, or you have a big devil and a little God." (Hagin Jr. p.56) What you think and say maters, it determines your destiny. You can walk in strong faith, or you can barely get by, the difference is in the believing. **Matthew 12:34 (KJV)**... *for out of the abundance of the heart the mouth speaketh.* Get it in your heart and your words will follow.

You already have that kind of faith in you. According to Romans 12:3 God has given all of us a measure of faith. If we did not have faith resident in us, we could not even get saved. **Ephesians 2:8 (KJV)** *8 For by grace are ye saved through faith; and that not of yourselves: it is the gift of God.* We do have faith, but some people develop their faith by using it.  I have muscles, but they are not well developed because I have not invested the time in weight lifting and such to make them stronger.  Some believers have highly developed faith, because they have used it repeatedly to lift greater and greater burdens.  We also know that we can build faith by focusing our attention on the Word of God.  **Romans 10:17 (KJV)** *17 So then faith cometh by hearing, and hearing by the word of God.*  Faith comes by hearing and hearing and hearing the Word of God until it is part of you, until it is the foundation you stand on.  Build yourself up on your most holy faith, read the word, listen to sermons and teachings until you are strong enough to cling to the promise and receive.  Learn it so well that you will speak it in the time of need.  **Romans 10:8-11 (KJV)** *8 But what saith it? The word is nigh thee, even in thy mouth, and in thy heart: that is, the word of faith, which we preach; 9 That if thou shalt confess with thy mouth the Lord Jesus, and shalt believe in thine heart that God hath raised him from the dead, thou shalt be saved. 10 For with the heart man believeth unto righteousness; and with the mouth confession is made unto salvation. 11 For the Scripture saith, Whosoever believeth on him shall not be ashamed.*  That is the faith formula.  Believe it in the heart and speak it with confidence.  It is the same process you used to get saved and it will accomplish whatever you need in life.

Get knowledge of God's will.  If you will hold on to what your heart says is true it will work.  "Faith will work in your heart with doubt in your head!" (Hagin p. 65)  It is what you believe in your heart that matters.  Our natural mind will argue with our spirit man, choose to listen to the Spirit and walk in steadfast obedience.  Of course there will be times your mind will want to doubt.  Just do not agree with your head; keep your mouth shut and the devil will not even know you had thoughts of doubt. Reinforce the truth until it makes a solid foundation and then just stand on it.

I heard a preacher tell this story one day. Early in a routine flight a pilot noticed a warning light on his control panel He left the cockpit to check and found that a door was slightly ajar. He prayed for the Lord to protect him and the flight crew. As he approached the door it flew open and he was sucked out of the plane. The copilot saw on the panel that the door was now open. He immediately turned the plane around and headed back to the airport and radioed for a helicopter to search the area for the lost pilot's body. After landing the plane everyone was astonished to find the pilot holding to a rung of the undercarriage of the plane that he had miraculously managed to grab. He had held on for fifteen minutes and even more amazing than that, he had managed to keep his head from hitting the runway only inches below him. When they got to the pilot they had to pry his fingers from the rung. That is perseverance. He held on with all his strength and more than likely a supernatural God given strength, because his life depended on it. He had prayed and he would not let go of God's protection even when all odds were against him. I am certain the devil made sure he thought it was possible that he would die. I am positive that he knew what would happen if he let go. That pilot just kept his grip tight because his life depended on it. That is how we stand in faith; we pray and we refuse to let go. **Galatians 6:9 (KJV)** *9 And let us not be weary in well doing: for in due season we shall reap, if we faint not.*

It is our part to make sure we know the truth, the Scriptures pertaining to our need. It is our part to be sure we are in right standing with God and free of sin. We go to Him and pray and then we trust in the One who bought us with His own blood. We do what we can to stand firm in faith until we get the answer to our prayers. **Ephesians 6:12-14 & 18 (KJV)** *12 For we wrestle not against flesh and blood, but against principalities, against powers, against the rulers of the darkness of this world, against spiritual wickedness in high places. 13 Wherefore take unto you the whole armour of God, that ye may be able to withstand in the evil day, and having done all, to stand. 14 Stand therefore, having your loins girt about with truth, and having on the breastplate of righteousness... 18 Praying always with all prayer and supplication in the Spirit, and watching thereunto with all perseverance and supplication for all saints;* There were times when I was willing to stand forever on what I believed and what I had asked. Usually if you are willing to stand forever, you do not have to stand very long before you get results.

Jesus no longer walks the earth, but He gave us power of attorney, we have the right to use His name. **John 16:23-24 (KJV)** *23 And in that day ye shall ask me nothing. Verily, verily, I say unto you, Whatsoever ye shall ask the Father in my name, he will give it you. 24 Hitherto have ye asked nothing in my name: ask, and ye shall receive, that your joy may be full.* When we pray in the name of Jesus it is just like He asked or prayed Himself. We use His authority. He said, "In that day..." He meant in the days after the resurrection, in the day when believers were born again. That day is this day. We use His name because it is endued with all of the same power and authority that was in the man Christ Jesus when He walked the earth. When my parents were first married, my mother walked into the bank and withdrew most of the money in my dad's account to pay for furniture. When asked why she thought she could do that she told them she was his wife. They understood her to be equal owner to the account, because she now bore his name. Using another's name is the legal right of those in the relationship. The true strength and power is in what is invested in the name of the one you represent. My mother is elderly and has Alzheimer's disease, so she is unable to manage her own finances. I was given power of attorney, which means I could cash in all of my mother's assets, make medical decisions and pay her bills as needed. I have access to all she owns, the only limitation I have is the amount invested in her name. I could not write a check for a million dollars because that is more than is in her account. **Mark 16:15-18 (KJV)** *15 And he said unto them, Go ye into all the world, and preach the gospel to every creature. 16 He that believeth and is baptized shall be saved; but he that believeth not shall be damned. 17 And these signs shall follow them that believe; <u>In my name</u> shall they cast out devils; they shall speak with new tongues; 18 They shall take up serpents; and if they drink any deadly thing, it shall not hurt them; they shall lay hands on the sick, and they shall recover.* Jesus gave us the right to use His name. **Luke 10:17 (KJV)** *17 And the seventy returned again with joy, saying, Lord, even the devils are subject unto us <u>through thy name</u>.* Miraculously, Jesus gave us full access and full authority to all He possesses and all He controls. Think about that, He who has a limitless supply gave us power of attorney. There is great power in the name of Jesus and we have the legal right to use it. **John 14:12-14 (KJV)** *12 Verily, verily, I say unto you, He that believeth on me, the works that I do shall he do also; and greater works than these shall he do; because I go unto my Father. 13 And whatsoever ye shall ask in my name, that will I do, that the Father may be glorified in the Son. 14 If ye shall ask any thing in my name, I will do it.*

It was the power invested in the name of Jesus that Peter used when he healed the lame man. **Acts 3:6 (KJV)** *6 Then Peter said, Silver and gold have I none; but such as I have give I thee: In the name of Jesus Christ of Nazareth rise up and walk.* Peter used the name of Jesus and a miracle occurred. He wrote a check on God's account and signed it with the name of Jesus and withdrew a miracle from the resources of heaven. **Acts 3:12-16 (KJV)** *12 And when Peter saw it, he answered unto the people, Ye men of Israel, why marvel ye at this? or why look ye so earnestly on us, as though by our own power or holiness we had made this man to walk? 13 The God of Abraham, and of Isaac, and of Jacob, the God of our fathers, hath glorified His Son Jesus; whom ye delivered up, and denied him in the presence of Pilate, when he was determined to let him go. 14 But ye denied the Holy One and the Just, and desired a murderer to be granted unto you; 15 And killed the Prince of life, whom God hath raised from the dead; whereof we are witnesses. 16 <u>And his name through faith in his name hath made this man strong</u>, whom ye see and know: yea, the faith which is by him hath given him this perfect soundness in the presence of you all.*

Rev. Essie Mae Carlisle was a woman of strong faith. It was a great honor to spend time in prayer with her. Before she died she stood in faith that all of her children would be saved. She had nine living children, and she lived to see some of them come to Christ. One of her sons became a preacher. One of her daughter-in-laws preaches conferences with me to this day. After she died, God continued to honor Granny Carlisle's prayer and we have seen the fruit of it. To date all but one of her children have been saved. I trust God that his day will come soon. She stood in faith, she believed and obeyed and God is still answering her prayers. To me, that sounds just like those people in the Hall of Faith, who died never having received the whole of their inheritance manifest. [Hebrews 11]

Every great hero of the faith had to step out and obey when they were neither capable in the flesh to live up to the call of God, nor had any evidence of success other than the word of God. They proved their love for the Lord by doing what He asked and today it the same. When we walk with Him in obedience it makes us eligible for the blessing. God demands that we walk in obedience and that requires faith, and produces the promises and blessings we receive. It may be a hard climb, but keep holding to that rope and putting one foot in front of the other. God has things for us we have not even imagined.

Psalm 50:15 *15 And call upon me in the day of trouble: I will deliver thee, and thou shalt glorify me.*

1 Corinthians 1:9 (KJV) *9 God is faithful...*

## Climbing is Hard

    Mountain climbing is hard. Spiritual climbing is hard too; it is not as easy as walking in faith. It is more like scaling Mt. Everest. It might seem like this struggle you are in today is the highest mountain in the world. The natural Everest has claimed hundreds of lives. All of those mountain climbers expected to make it to the top or they would not have tried, but there were obstacles along the way. Some ridges were higher than expected, the air got thin, and then the ice made death a real possibility. The reason why people climb is personal. They want the challenge, or they have something to prove. Some want to be among that small group who have faced the mountain and come down stronger for the climb. They faced their mortality and overcame great hardship. In every case there was struggle and pain. It is that way in the spirit too. We want to draw near to God, but sometimes that path seems nearly impossible.

    I asked God once about my own prayer and praise life. He said the best worship I ever gave Him was not when I sang a solo at church, or preached or taught a class. It was not when I wept in His presence or danced in the spirit. My best praise did not come during any formal worship or even at the church. I gave my best offering of praise in an ICU room where my 12 year old daughter lay in a coma, as I softly sang a short chorus about standing on Jesus, the rock of my salvation. That song did not feel anointed, or sound especially good. It felt like I was struggling to climb a near vertical face of a towering mountain, but I was putting one foot in front of the other. I was holding fast to every rock and crevice and reaching for the next.

It was September 22, 1988. My youngest daughter, Amy, was twelve years old, and we were driving to school. It was just another day. We were talking about moving to a new house and she was laughing about getting a room with a better view than her older sister. She wanted a tissue, and the box had slid under the seat. She could not reach it, so she unhooked her seatbelt, just for a second and bent over. Then everything changed. Several cars ahead someone looked away from the road to adjust their radio. They ran into the car in front of them. They were hit by the truck behind them. Then the driver in the car behind the truck crashed into it. The driver of the shiny new Firebird in front of me never even had time to step on the brake. I did not have time to stop either. My foot pushed the brake to the floor but it was too late. I remember screaming the name of Jesus. When the sound of crunching metal stopped and all I could hear was a constant alarm going off, I looked into the passenger seat. There was my precious daughter, her body contorted in a seizure, her eyes rolled back in her head. She was unconscious. I remember getting out of the car and going around to her side, I wanted to immobilize her neck, in case she had broken it. On the way around the car, I yelled for someone to call 911. Then with no one on earth listening I said firmly, "Devil you cannot have my daughter." I also talked with my Lord while I knelt there holding her head between my hands. I remember speaking directly to Him,

"Lord if you want her, I will give her to you. If there is any way you can give her back to me, I want her to live, but don't leave her like this. Make her whole or take her with you." I meant all of those words. Deep in my heart I knew it was going to be a hard climb.

When the first fireman arrived he took my place and started an IV there was very little blood in the car. It came from a cut on the back of her head. Amy's face looked perfect; on the outside she was mostly undamaged. She had a second seizure, and we all suspected a brain injury. The ambulance arrived shortly after they had placed a neck brace on her and started moving her to a backboard. The EMT seemed in a big hurry and asked which hospital. I asked him which was best and he said, "Right now all that matters is which is closest." So we went to St. Anthony's.

When we arrived they did an exam on me while they did CT scans and such on Amy. They said the best Neurosurgeon in town 'just happened' to be in the hospital. The doctor said she had two cerebral hemorrhages, and she had less than an hour to live without surgery. So my husband and I signed consent forms and they rushed her into an operating room. It was five hours later when we got the first report, and another two before the surgery was completed. The surgeon took us into a conference room and told us her chances were not good. If she made it through the day, we would see if she ever woke up. If she did wake up, his belief was that she would basically be a vegetable. "If she wakes we will find out if she can see, or think, or hear or move." His words were not encouraging. He said they had drilled three holes in her skull and then cut out a circle of bone about the size of an orange to reduce the pressure from the hemorrhage on the side of her brain. The second cerebral hemorrhage was on the back of her head and it was inoperable. If the swelling in her brain subsided, she could come out of the coma in about three days. It was too dangerous to try to airlift her to a children's hospital. So there lay my little girl, the youngest person who had ever been in the ICU at St. Anthony's Hospital. They told us what to expect, there would be wires and several monitors and a ventilator to breath for her. She had a probe sticking out of her head, reading brain pressure. They had to shave off most of her hair, but they kept it in a bag to send to the funeral parlor later. She had a feeding tube in her nose, three IV's and a catheter. None of those words even began to tell how bad it looked when we walked into that room. She looked so small and frail, but at least her face was not contorted and her hands were not knotted into claws. They let my husband and I stay for less than 5 minutes. They said the sound of our footsteps made her brain swell and that the pressure was her greatest danger. The next twenty-four hours were critical. Everyone I knew was praying. There were at least twenty people from the church and my family in the waiting room most of the time.

Three hours later, Amy sat up in bed and tried to pull out the tube in her nose and the one down her throat. She tried with her right hand first and when she could not reach it because her hands were tied to the bedrails, she tried with her left. To me that showed reasoning, and she was semi-conscious; they immediately sedated her. There was some hope, but the nurses said not to get too excited just yet. Amy drifted in and out of a medically induced coma. Her brain pressure went up and down. When the pressure was low, we were allowed ten minutes an hour in her room. When it was high we could watch her from behind a window. It was in one of those low pressure times, in the wee hours of the morning that I stood at the foot of her bed singing softly. *Praise the name of Jesus, praise the name of Jesus, He's my rock, He's my fortress, He is my deliverer. In Him will I trust, praise the name of Jesus ...* I did not know that was my finest praise. I wanted Amy surrounded by the Word, and faith, not listening to the doom the doctors and nurses spoke over her. Eventually they let me put a tape player in her room with praise music day and night but that night it was just my feeble voice and my confidence in the Lord I trusted with her life.

We camped out in that ICU waiting room twenty-four hours a day. I did my praying in the waiting room bathroom. I would go in all alone and whisper to the only One who could do anything to save her. It was there in that bathroom floor that God gave me a Scripture to hang on to. **Isaiah 50:4 (KJV**) *4 The Lord GOD hath given me the tongue of the learned, that I should know how to speak a word in season to him that is weary: he wakeneth morning by morning, he wakeneth mine ear to hear as the learned.* I took that to mean Amy would wake up and that she would have a normal mind and she would both hear and speak. I clung to that word from God. It was my anchor, driven deep into the bedrock of Scripture as Amy and I hung on a lifeline over the gaping abyss.

On the third day, she was more active. I told the nurse, "I am a sign language interpreter, and Amy knows a little sign. If she wakes up and can't talk because of all those tubes, she will try to sign. When she does, call me." She smiled and acted like I was crazy. Later that day, she called me. Amy was moving her hand and when the nurse asked if she was signing and wanted her mom, Amy nodded. I walked into the room, her eyes were still a little hazy but I talked to her and she started spelling out these words, "Am I going to die?" When I said no, she spelled, "Can I have a drink of water?" When the nurse said no, Amy started to cry and they sedated her again. But that nurse went out in the hall and jumped up and down with me. In the morning when the surgeon made his rounds, he asked me to explain exactly what had happened. I told him that Amy rarely signed, and she had spelled out letter by letter the two sentences. He said that was good because at least she could talk with her mother, because she was very unlikely to be able to speak. The injury had been near the speech center of the brain. Again, he gave me a negative report, and again I held to that word in Isaiah

She was in the ICU for nine days. When she was breathing on her own and the tubes came out she could speak in a whisper. They moved her to a regular room for another five days. God had been faithful. There were still a few peaks to climb. Some of her memories were scrambled. For example, she could not remember her sister was named Marie, so she called her "sixteen," which was her age. Near the end of our hospital stay she had quadruple vision, but she could see. When her vision corrected itself enough she could read words like "encyclopedia" but not small words like "the, and, or it." Those site words had to be relearned, so did her multiplication tables. Her balance was off for a short time, but she could walk. When we went for her post-surgery checkup, the surgeon said the second blood clot had mysteriously dissolved. I knew the Lord had removed it. The Surgeon said, "You must have a purpose to be here; you should not have lived. Make something good out of your life." He wanted her on anti-seizure medicine but she asked me, "Mom did God heal me or not?" When I said yes, she refused to take it. She never did have a seizure.

Today, Amy is forty. She is the mother of four amazing children. She has two degrees and she works as an occupational therapist assistant. She is perfect and whole. She has a scar shaped like a "question mark" on one side of her head and a second the size of a quarter on the back. Fortunately, she has lots of hair to cover them. If you feel her skull there are dents about like the finger holes in a bowling ball. The drill holes never fill in, but the circle of bone was reinserted and grew back fine. Amy is my miracle child. She taught me to trust God while climbing a very steep ridge. **Psalm 50:15 (KJV)** *15 And call upon me in the day of trouble: I will deliver thee, and thou shalt glorify me.* God was and is faithful—to Him be all the glory.

He was a stronghold, a fortress when I had my deepest need. **Psalm 86:5-7 (KJV)** *5 For thou, Lord, art good, and ready to forgive; and plenteous in mercy unto all them that call upon thee. 6 Give ear, O LORD, unto my prayer; and attend to the voice of my supplications. 7 In the day of my trouble I will call upon thee: for thou wilt answer me.* In my day of trouble, I asked for a miracle and I got it.

Climbing toward God in the time of crisis is one of the hardest things we ever do. It is also the only way out most of the time. **Matthew 7:7-8 (KJV)** *7 Ask, and it shall be given you; seek, and ye shall find; knock, and it shall be opened unto you: 8 For every one that asketh receiveth; and he that seeketh findeth; and to Him that knocketh it shall be opened.* You do not want to just quietly wait it out. Pray to Him and He will answer you. Actively seek Him and He will help you. Worship Him and He will turn His face toward you. You will find God faithful during the hardest climbs of your life. He will be your companion and your strength if you will call upon Him.

**Psalm 18:30-33 (KJV)** *30 As for God, His way is perfect: the word of the LORD is tried: he is a buckler to all those that trust in him. 31 For who is God save the LORD? Or who is a rock save our God? 32 It is God that girdeth me with strength, and maketh my way perfect. 33 He maketh my feet like hinds' feet, and setteth me upon my high places.* On the steepest slopes, The Lord will make you stand secure; He will keep you from falling. There is safety in His presence. No matter how hard the climb is, He is with us and He is more than enough.

Luke 9:35 35 *And there came a voice out of the cloud, saying, This is my beloved Son: hear him.*

MEET ME ON THE MOUNTAIN

## Mt. of Transfiguration
## A Glimpse of the Glory

Just before they saw this manifestation of the Glory, two important things happened. First Peter spoke by the Spirit that Jesus was the Christ, the Messiah. At which point Jesus confirmed that upon that revelation, He would build His church and then Jesus told them that He was about to be crucified and rise from the dead. Those two great revelations were a prerequisite to this time alone with them on the mountain.

Peter, James and John were on a precipice they had not climbed before. Those three disciples did not know they were about to experience something of great magnitude. They only knew that Jesus left most of His followers behind and withdrew to the mountain. It was a private place. It was customary for Jesus to pull away and pray. They may have thought that was all that would happen, but it was always an honor to go with Him to prayer. **Matthew 17:1-8 (KJV)** *1 And after six days Jesus taketh Peter, James, and John His brother, and bringeth them up into an high mountain apart,*

This was His inner circle, those who knew Him best. They alone went in when the Lord raised Jairus' daughter and they were the ones called to watch with Him at Gethsemane. Their prior relationship made them eligible for greater revelation and deeper experiences. *2 And was transfigured before them: and His face did shine as the sun, and His raiment was white as the light. 3 And, behold, there appeared unto them Moses and Elias talking with Him.* There was a drastic change in His appearance; actually the original word was almost the same as our word metamorphosis. His image was so changed that it revealed something of His glory. He was not revealing all that He was in heaven, but it was more than any earthly man could grasp of the nature and character of God. That light was not from outside of Jesus but rather emanated from within Him. When faced with the supernatural manifestation of the glory, people should usually keep their mouth shut and just observe and receive. Peter was not the type to stand there quietly. *4 Then answered Peter, and said unto Jesus, Lord, it is good for us to be here: if thou wilt, let us make here three tabernacles; one for thee, and one for Moses, and one for Elias.* Peter let this moment in the glory shake him up. He saw the one who represented the Law and the one who represented the prophets and he did not think it strange to put Jesus on the same level. Jesus however, was so much more than a prophet or a teacher or a leader. He was indeed the Son of God.

Peter had said "You are the Christ" but this One who walked with them was far more than any of the disciples really knew. It is interesting to me that Peter recognized these two men who had died so long before he was born. He knew who they were and recognized their place in history and in the spirit world. All that was ever known about the coming of the Messiah, and His purpose was recorded, by either Moses or the prophets. Peter did not just sit there and listen to them. He did not wait to hear from Jesus. Instead of seeking more of the glory he wanted to build a shrine to remember it. Just like Peter we sometimes want to set up camp at the place of our last encounter with God. We are willing to get stagnant by staying there. We like that good memory so we want to memorialize it; we would build a monument and stay there. We sing that same song that we were singing when He showed up last time. We look to the same minister who was preaching or praying when the whole time it is not the song, the preacher or anything of this earth. What our hearts cry for is more of God. Keep climbing there is more of God than you could ever imagine. *5 While he yet spake, behold, a bright cloud overshadowed them: and behold a voice out of the cloud, which said, This is my beloved Son, in whom I am well pleased;* Those were the same words God spoke when Jesus was baptized. *This is my beloved Son, in whom I am well pleased; hear ye Him. 6 And when the disciples heard it, they fell on their face, and were sore afraid.* I tend to think that God was talking with Jesus about the cross and the resurrection. The words these disciples were witness to were very important. It was His coming sacrificial death that mattered, not their experience. God did not want them distracted from what was ultimately His plan to save the world. [See Luke 9:28-36] The spectacular is often so distracting it takes away from the supernatural. This experience was meant to reveal hidden truth to them. It would be a source of strength and understanding when Jesus actually died. I am not sure they took hold of the revelation offered in the way they were intended to receive it. The value of any vision or encounter with God is the results. Did it change you? Did it give you new understanding or greater hunger? We have no information on how it affected them, but we do know that they wrote about it later. The main recipient in this supernatural encounter must have been Jesus, who was about to face the sin of all mankind and the pressure of bearing it without any pulling away. He had to walk into hell in our place. These two men were sent to talk with Him and surely their message was of great value to our Lord. The disciples seem to have been in a state of semi-consciousness, *7 And Jesus came and touched them, and said, Arise, and be not afraid. 8 And when they had lifted up their eyes, they saw no man, save Jesus only.* They had missed some of what Jesus wanted them to know and then they became overwhelmed by the voice of God. They had been in the presence of the glory. What they saw and heard was more than any of the other disciples had experienced. I am sure they talked with one another and with Jesus about what had happened there. After a while, they left the place of their encounter and the quiet of the mountain. No matter how great the experience, they still had to return to their daily lives.

Most of the time when we have a really impactiful, spiritual encounter with God, we find Him in a quiet place. We need intimate time on our own mountain with God. We need to set our sights on things above. We need time to revive our spirits. After we have been nurtured and strengthen and received from God, we are ready to walk among men again.

## Sitting down on the path

    We might be sitting down on the path instead of climbing. When we came to pray, we thought we were seeking His face, and climbing. In truth we often became distracted. We have been busy with work, and family obligations and even the church. We have plenty to do each day, all of those responsibilities crept into our minds while trying to pray. Are we in denial? Thinking that all is fine while it is not? Do we attend church without attending to the Spirit? Have we grown stagnant, complacent, and aloof when He has called us to intimacy? Have we denied Him with our words or actions or the coldness of our hearts? Have we sat by in silence when we should have declared our love for Him? Have we grown indifferent? Then, we are no better disciple than Peter the night Jesus was arrested. We have become part of the world around us. We have been asleep when He called us to watch with Him and pray with Him. Our flesh is weak and we gladly yielded to it. Are our hearts so cold we have to ask "Is it I?" It is time to do a progress check and if we are not climbing, we need to get back at it.

    On the night Jesus was betrayed, He sat at a religious gathering with the ones who followed Him most closely.

They were gathered to celebrate the Passover, but it was to be their last supper. **Mark 14:18-21 (KJV)** *18 And as they sat and did eat, Jesus said, Verily I say unto you, One of you which eateth with me shall betray me.* What a sad revelation. Here they are gathered to eat the best meal they have had in a long time. No one is currently attacking them or demanding their master's time and attention. No one is clamoring for a healing touch, and yet He says they will turn away. Could that even be possible? *19 And they began to be sorrowful, and to say unto Him one by one, Is it I? and another said, Is it I?* Peter thinks and then says, "If everyone else deserts you, I will stand by you; I am willing to die for you." These are the bold words of one feasting in a place of safety. Like us, Peter thinks he stands firm. He knows Jesus. He has seen the Lord's power and felt His presence and he thinks I'm solid, but the pressure was about to come and he would fail. *20 And he answered and said unto them, It is one of the twelve, that dippeth with me in the dish. 21 The Son of man indeed goeth, as it is written of him: but woe to that man by whom the Son of man is betrayed! good were it for that man if he had never been born.* The disciples think, one of us, sitting right here will betray Him and it will lead to His death. What a horrible way to ruin our time with Him. It would not be me, would it? It is hard to come closer to Christ if you don't notice you have strayed. When does hot become warm and warm become cool? It is slight changes, almost undetectable. Each of them thinks it cannot be me.

**Mark 14:22-25 (KJV)** *22 And as they did eat, Jesus took bread, and blessed, and brake it, and gave to them, and said, Take, eat: this is my body. 23 And he took the cup, and when he had given thanks, he gave it to them: and they all drank of it. 24 And he said unto them, This is my blood of the new testament, which is shed for many. 25 Verily I say unto you, I will drink no more of the fruit of the vine, until* *that day that I drink it new in the kingdom of God.* Holy Communion was established in the middle of this discourse about betrayal and sorrow about His upcoming death. Jesus reached into the basket of bread, picked up that middle piece of flatbread. The disciples always thought the three loaves were representative of the patriarchs, Abraham, Isaac and Jacob. Instead they represented the Trinity. They were stacked like pancakes, the Father, the Son, and the Holy Spirit. He takes that middle one and says this is my body and He cracks it open, tears it in half and passes it to be eaten. Then He takes the cup of the Messiah, the one never used at the table, and fills it with wine. He says this is my blood. They catch just a glimpse of the enormity of it, the horror of His blood being poured out. He says drink it. Make my death and my life a part of you. Be filled with me, become my covenant partners. It has become a solemn thing. They drink, but they do not grasp the fullness of what they do. We sit at the communion table and eat and drink too. Do we enter into the experience of His death and resurrection? Do we identify with the one who died there on the cross for us and cherish the blood shed? Do we grasp the fullness of our guilt and shame that sent Him to die? Do we celebrate the fact that we are redeemed with precious blood and in so doing, honor Him?

**Mark 14:26-31 (KJV)** *26 And when they had sung an hymn, they went out into the mount of Olives.* They went about church as usual, that is what it was you know. People gathered because they claimed to know the Lord. People like us were partaking of communion, and listening to His words and then singing hymns. They were in close proximity to the Master, but only God knows what was going on in each of their hearts. *27 And Jesus saith unto them, All ye shall be offended because of me this night: for it is written, I will smite the shepherd, and the sheep shall be scattered.* They were shocked, Jesus would be arrested and they would be dispersed; the small body of believers was under attack. *28 But after that I am risen, I will go before you into Galilee. 29 But Peter said unto Him, Although all shall be offended, yet will not I.* That sounds like all of us. I am strong, and I love you and I would never do such a thing...and then like Peter we deny Him with our words or actions. *30 And Jesus saith unto Him, Verily I say unto thee, That this day, even in this night, before the cock crow twice, thou shalt deny me thrice. 31 But he spake the more vehemently, If I should die with thee, I will not deny thee in any wise. Likewise also said they all.* No one intends to betray Him, or deny Him, but sometimes we get tired and we just sit down on the path for a while. Sometimes we let the passion in us grow cold and stagnant and then we are easy prey and our flesh takes over and we just act without forethought.

**Mark 14:32-40 (KJV)** *32 And they came to a place which was named Gethsemane:* It wasn't their first time in that garden. They had come to pray other times too. After all, Jesus was frequently in prayer. *and he saith to His disciples, Sit ye here, while I shall pray. 33 And he taketh with Him Peter and James and John, and began to be sore amazed, and to be very heavy; 34 And saith unto them, My soul is exceeding sorrowful unto death: tarry ye here, and watch.* He did not really tell them to pray, more to just lend their moral support while He struggled against the weight of man's sin. They could not have understood what He faced. They did not know Jesus was about to embrace every foul sin of mankind and die in their stead. He just stepped away a short distance and began to pray while they sat in silence and wondered over the events of the day. *35 And he went forward a little, and fell on the ground, and prayed that, if it were possible, the hour might pass from Him. 36 And he said, Abba, Father, all things are possible unto thee; take* *away this cup from me: nevertheless not what I will, but what thou wilt.* When Jesus spoke of drinking from the cup, it was the cup of the covenant. If there was any other means of redemption it would have been offered, but there was not. Jesus entered into covenant with the Father to take on all the sins of mankind, embracing the filth of the world that separated God and man. Jesus did not sweat blood over the pain He would face. Man's fallen nature and the enormity of sin that He must embody caused Him to struggle. The Holy One of Israel became sin for us. All that was evil would fit inside the Son of God and be carried before the spirit world where sin would be judged. Jesus knew He would become separated from God the Father for the first time since eternity began. Spiritual death would claim a third of the Trinity. He would walk into hell in our place. This was the cup of the covenant that Jesus must drink if man went free. *37 And he cometh, and findeth them sleeping, and saith unto Peter, Simon, sleepest thou? couldest not thou watch one hour?* One hour doesn't sound like much. We would give the Lord one hour, right? We would pray that long, and worship that long. We would never short change Him or make a shopping list in our head during our quiet time with Him, would we? *38 Watch ye and pray, lest ye enter into temptation. The spirit truly is ready, but the flesh is weak. 39 And again he went away, and prayed, and spake the same words. 40 And when he returned, he found them asleep again, (for their eyes were heavy,) neither wist they what to answer Him.* There are no words to adequately say I did not pray when I should have. There are no words that say I am not that good of a friend to you Jesus. They had no answer. We have no answer.

The truth is they did arrest Jesus that night. Peter tried to be bold and strong, but honestly Jesus did not intend for this to be a sword fight and He had to shut Peter down. The Master was taken, and every disciple fled. Peter hung out just a short physical distance off from the Lord and warmed himself by the enemy's fire. He took an interest in what the outcome would be but did not put himself out too much. He had a wait and see attitude. The man of commitment seems missing. The man of action from the garden where he swung his sword has cowered in fear. Every compromise pulls him farther into the shadows and he is now sitting in the court of the enemy, undetected. His very presence there is a denial of his connection to the Lord. He is too near the natural fire to burn with a fire within.

When confronted by a young girl with no status or power he denies knowing Jesus and then someone else sees him and says weren't you there in the garden and he more strongly denies it. Later when the men press upon him, and they are beginning to draw attention to him and there is some real danger he denies the Lord a third time and curses and swears and then the rooster crows. Peter remembered the words Jesus, *"Before the cock crow, thou shalt deny me thrice."* The Bible tells us Peter went out, and wept bitterly.

Peter didn't have to follow from far off. It might have been better for him if he had just run away like the other disciples did. They had all been cowards, but they did not have to live with what he spoke, the vocal denial, or the lie about his allegiance. It was probably easier for them to repent. Like Peter we don't usually fall into vile sin, but we get too comfortable in the Lord's presence and we lose that sense of awe. Like Peter we are grateful but distanced. While Jesus prepares to climb Mount Calvary, we dawdle, following at leisure from a place apart. We, like Peter, are getting too much in the flesh and warming ourselves in the comfort of the nearest fire—casual in our faith until we nearly deny Him ourselves.

Jesus gave us instructions about our place in this world too. **Matthew 5:14-16 (KJV)** *14 Ye are the light of the world. A city that is set on an hill cannot be hid. 15 Neither do men light a candle, and put it under a bushel, but on a candlestick; and it giveth light unto all that are in the house. 16 Let your light so shine before men, that they may see your good works, and glorify your Father which is in heaven.* He also said that we were to go into the entire world and preach the gospel. He said we were to be His representatives, His witnesses. Sometimes we just want to fit in; it is almost like we are wearing camo. Where is the light of the world? If He is so alive in us why don't we shine with His glory? We won't have to warm ourselves by the fire of the world if the Fire of God is burning inside us.

**Romans 8:35 (KJV)** *35 Who shall separate us from the love of Christ? shall tribulation, or distress, or persecution, or famine, or nakedness, or peril, or sword? Romans 8:38-39 (KJV) 38 For I am persuaded, that neither death, nor life, nor angels, nor principalities, nor powers, nor things present, nor things to come, 39 Nor height, nor depth, nor any other creature, shall be able to separate us from the love of God, which is in Christ Jesus our Lord.* Nothing from outside of us can harm us or pull us away, but what is in our hearts? We have to purposefully, daily choose to walk with Him. We have to intentionally climb to be near Him.

**Galatians 6:7-9 (KJV)** *7 Be not deceived; God is not mocked: for whatsoever a man soweth, that shall he also reap. 8 For he that soweth to his flesh shall of the flesh reap corruption; but he that soweth to the Spirit shall of the Spirit reap life everlasting. 9 And let us not be weary in well doing: for in due season we shall reap, if we faint not.* Where are we? Do we live for the spirit or the flesh? We can be warmed by the fire of God or look to the comforts of the world. Just how close are we following Christ? God has called us to walk with Him to climb with Him. He only demands two things, passion and obedience. He cries out for us to draw near; He wants relationship, fellowship, and deep spiritual communion with us.

**James 4:7-10 (KJV)** *7 Submit yourselves therefore to God. Resist the devil, and he will flee from you. 8 Draw nigh to God, and he will draw nigh to you. Cleanse your hands, ye sinners; and purify your hearts, ye double minded. 9 Be afflicted, and mourn, and weep: let your laughter be turned to mourning, and your joy to heaviness. 10 Humble yourselves in the sight of the Lord, and he shall lift you up.* We choose how close we are to God. We surrender ourselves completely to Him—or not. We stay filled with His fire and His presence or we walk completely away or we follow from afar. We choose that.

That is why Jesus calls us to walk in passion and communion and to climb closer and closer to Him. He wants us with Him. He wants us burning with love and filled with His glory. We can never be what He wants or do what He said if we just sit down where we are. We have to get up and start climbing again.

## MEET ME ON THE MOUNTAIN

### *It is worth the climb*

Have you ever been mountain climbing? Right after Amy was born we went to California to visit my in-laws. My sister-law and her husband wanted to take us hiking. I remember telling them, "Look I just had a baby; I am not in shape for anything rough." They assured us that we would just be climbing a few small hills. I asked if we needed any equipment and they said no. So the next morning when they arrived I was wearing my smooth bottomed tennis shoes, and they were wearing serious hiking boots. As we drove closer I could see more than hills and then they turned into an area that was posted San Bernardino Mountains. I was doomed. We climbed for hours over rocks and shale that slid from under our feet and we were trusting Bob to keep us safe. Eventually Bob disappeared. We didn't know what had happened to him. I imagined him lying in the bottom of some ravine with broken limbs. He had told us in the beginning that if anyone got lost, the rest would stick to the original destination, which only Bob and Charmaine knew. He was gone for hours and we were just sticking to the path, and hoping to find a forest ranger to go look for him. We were climbing higher and higher. In my mind I remember thinking this is what the survivors of airplane crashes feel like when they are hiking out of the mountains looking for help. Eventually, we found Bob. We reached the summit and we looked over the top of the waterfall to see the people who were resting hundreds of feet below. It made for some cool pictures. I never really wanted to go again. To me that was enough climbing in the natural to last a lifetime.

It is beautiful to walk on those low lying hills, and the higher you go the more beautiful it is, but it gets rougher too. That happens in the spirit as well. The path that others have traveled is well-worn and easy to follow. As you continue to climb, the way gets steep and narrow, there is underbrush in the way and it feels like you can never make it to that place you are seeking, but you can.

**2 Samuel 22:29-34 (KJV)** *29 For thou art my lamp, O LORD: and the LORD will lighten my darkness. 30 For by thee I have run through a troop: by my God have I leaped over a wall. 31 As for God, his way is perfect; the word of the LORD is tried: he is a buckler to all them that trust in him. 32 For who is God, save the LORD? and who is a rock, save our God? 33 God is my strength and power: and he maketh my way perfect. 34 He maketh my feet like hinds' feet: and setteth me upon my high places.* God makes us able to climb the steepest hills. Sometimes it just gets hard, and it feels like we are lost and have used up all our resources but God is faithful and He will make us overcomers. He has traveled this path before and He knows the way out. As long as we keep following Him, we will not be lost, and we will not fall.

**Romans 8:37-39 (KJV)** *37 Nay, <u>in all these things we are more than conquerors through Him that loved us</u>. 38 For I am persuaded, that neither death, nor life, nor angels, nor principalities, nor powers, nor things present, nor things to come, 39 Nor height, nor depth, nor any other creature, shall be able to separate us from the love of God, which is in Christ Jesus our Lord.*

Remember what happened with Elijah on Mount Horeb. **1 Kings 19:11 (KJV)** *11 And he said, Go forth, and stand upon the mount before the LORD.* There were several manifestations before God came to him in a whisper quite, "still small voice." We know that God spoke softly to Elijah and helped him to understand the things to come and got him through this time of struggle. Like him we need to recognize that we will have highs and lows and in both of them God is present. We need to push aside all else and climb to the place where there are no more distractions, so we can hear Him clearly. Like Elijah, we need to respond when we first hear the faint voice of the spirit, so He can continue to minister to us. Until we act on what we have heard, we will hear no more.

When Buzz and I were married about eight months, I got saved. Eventually, he went to church with me, but his commitment was nominal. We moved to a new town around six years later and in 1980 I fell deeply in love with Jesus. I was baptized in the Holy Spirit and started going to a non-denominational church. Let's just say there was strong resistance to my new relationship with God. Buzz started drinking more, and I could not go with him to bars. He was traveling one path and I was going another. There were five long years of fighting, and silence and bitterness. He left several times. First he was gone for a weekend, later he disappeared for a few weeks. He came and went as he pleased. One time when he came home, he indicated that he had found a deeper place of faith. Nothing really changed. Once he took a three week vacation to California without the rest of us. He continued his love affair with beer and I ravenously consumed the Word. Buzz grew more and more bitter. He slept in the family room in the basement for about six months. Eventually, he totally moved out. This time he was gone for months, and he asked for a divorce. I was broken and while he thought the problem was my pastor or my church. I told him, "That's not fair. You aren't asking me to choose you over a person or a place, you want me to choose you over God and I can't do that."

I lost all respect for my husband, and my feelings for him were very weak. One night as I prayed, I asked God to love Buzz through me. I said. "I don't think I have any love left, please give me your love for him." I did not expect for the marriage to ever be whole again. I asked for God to help me. I remember praying for his soul but not his love. Finally, I told God, "If he is never going to love me or love you then go ahead and take him out of my life so it won't hurt so much." I turned it all over to God. It was months of silence. Buzz came to see the girls, and took them out for fun visits. He paid the house payment and the utilities, but nothing more. I had never worked outside of the home, but I had to get a job and it was hard going through all the turmoil and working. I remember not having enough money to buy a jar of peanut butter. I was so hurt and so lonely. I was trusting God but every day was a struggle.

One day when I was finally getting used to being alone and had resigned myself to his desire to divorce me, Buzz came by to visit. He was not there for the girls; he came to see me. He came in while I was cleaning up the shreds of what had been my bedroom carpet. The dog was not adjusting well to being alone so much so she took out her frustrations on about a yard of carpet near the door. I was crying when Buzz walked in. I said, "I can't afford new carpet and we can't even sell the house looking like this." He told me he would buy the carpet. He had been really tight with money so that made me curious. He asked for a date. Just dinner and a Bible study. A Bible study, really? That did not sound like my husband. After a while he told me that he had spent a lot of time thinking. He was sitting in a bar one night and came to a realization, "I thought coming here made me happy, but no one is happy here." Then he went back to his tiny apartment and dug out the Bible I had slipped into his suitcase. He said, "Kathy always found an answer here." He started to read and hours later he started to pray. He told me he spent the whole night asking God to forgive him for what he he had done to me. He poured out all of his alcohol. He told me, "I don't know what to call it, but one minute I was on a train going left and the next I was on a train headed right." He had played the, 'I got saved' card before so I didn't really trust his new found love for God and me. When I was praying I asked God what to do, I was just getting used to living alone, and I didn't want to let him back into my heart just to be hurt again. God gave me a Scripture by reference, in Job. I never really liked Job and didn't know what it said until I looked. **Job 11:10 (KJV)** *10 If he cut off, and shut up, or gather together, then who can hinder him?* I took that to mean that God would work it out His way and I could not change the outcome. So we had a long talk and I told Buzz all the things that I needed to say. He just listened, really listened and he said I was right. We dated for a few weeks and the change was real. I knew he really was not the man who had hurt me so deeply. That man was dead, crucified with Christ and this was a new man proclaiming his love for me. Buzz bought me an engagement ring and we went to my pastor who Buzz had so resented and asked him to renew our vows, because frankly they had been broken.

That was about thirty-five years ago. God healed our marriage so perfectly it is as if it didn't even happen to us. I almost feel like I watched it in a movie or read it in a book. Today, my husband is a godly man and a tower of support for our pastor. He is on the church board and faithful in attendance, and giving and he ministers on the worship teem. We are really happily married and I treasure him as a gift from God. It was a long, hard climb but it was worth it. God was faithful and we can look back and see His hand reaching down to both of us to lift us closer to Him.

The pastor who married us told us that marriage takes three. God and man and woman are each is on one point of an equilateral triangle. If the man and woman really want to be closer to each other, they travel toward God. He was right. Union with God and each other is a strong bond. **Matthew 19:5-6 (KJV)** *5 And said, For this cause shall a man leave father and mother, and shall cleave to his wife: and they twain shall be one flesh? 6 Wherefore they are no more twain, but one flesh. What therefore God hath joined together, let not man put asunder.* God had invested in our marriage and with His help we could stand united again.

**2 Timothy 1:12 (KJV)** *12 For the which cause I also suffer these things: nevertheless I am not ashamed: for I know whom I have believed, and am persuaded that he is able to keep that which I have committed unto him against that day.* I had committed my home and family into the faithful hands of my Lord and even though it seemed like we were sliding downhill fast, God kept us safe and made us whole again.

**2 Timothy 2:19 (KJV)** *19 Nevertheless the foundation of God standeth sure, having this seal, The Lord knoweth them that are his. And, Let every one that nameth the name of Christ depart from iniquity.* We do well to become completely dependent upon God who can and will guide and direct us. He knows us better than we know ourselves. He

knew the man my husband would become and that man was well suited for the climb I am on now.

**Galatians 6:8-9 (KJV)** *8 For he that soweth to his flesh shall of the flesh reap corruption; but he that soweth to the Spirit shall of the Spirit reap life everlasting. 9 And <u>let us not be weary in well doing: for in due season we shall reap, if we faint not</u>.* Everything about meeting with God is based on who He is. It is all about His holiness and His willingness to meet with us. Every desire to draw near comes from Him. He yearns for His children to come to Him—day by day the Lord is waiting for us to fellowship with Him. We need to recognize the glory that there is in just knowing Him. He is calling us unto Himself, *"Come unto me all you who are weary and I will give you rest."* He is calling us into deeper and more powerful encounters. God wants us to climb constantly towards Him. He is preparing us for eternity upon heavenly mountains, but for now we get to visit from time to time.

In the spirit, just like in the natural, the higher you go the rougher the terrain. There is a well-worn path in the lowlands. Many have walked in the foot hills. The path is not well defined when you move past a certain point. You create your own path by the time you are half way up the mountain. God is calling us higher and higher. He is reaching out His hand to us to help us over the roughest rocks and canyons. He is calling to us, to you and to me with urgency and passion. He is saying "Come meet me on the mountain."

# Works Cited

John Bevere, Drawing Near, (Nashville, TN, Thomas Nelson Publishers, 2004) p.2, 4, 11, 13, 22, 50, 111, 117, 119.

Kenneth E. Hagin, Mountain Moving Faith, (Tulsa, OK, Rhema Bible Church, 1993) p. 4, 65.

Kenneth Hagin Jr., Speak to Your Mountain, (Tulsa, OK, Rhema Bible Church, 1993) p. 56, 83, 88, 103.

E. W. Kenyon, In His Presence, (Lynnwood, Washington, Kenyon's Gospel Publishing Society, 1969), p. 81, 88, 106, 117, 200, 218.

Marshall, Morgan and Scott, Matthew Henry's Commentary on the Whole Bible in One Volume, (Grand Rapids, MI, Zondervan, 1960) .

Derek Prince, Entering the Presence of God, (Kensington KY, Whitaker House, 2007) p. 16, 23, 29, 36, 128.

Malcolm Smith, The Lost Secret of the New Covenant, (Tulsa, OK: Harrison House, 2002), p. 27, 138.

James Strong, Strong's Exhaustive Concordance of the Bible, (Nashville, TN: Royal Publisher, Inc., 1979)

Maxwell Whyte, The power of the Blood, (New Kensington, PA: Whitaker House, 1973), p.14.

Unless otherwise indicated, all Scripture References are from the King James Version of the Bible

# MEET ME ON THE MOUNTAIN

www.ingramcontent.com/pod-product-compliance
Lightning Source LLC
Chambersburg PA
CBHW071735080526
44588CB00013B/2044